"McPhie and Smith have penned a book that addresses one of the most critical issues of our time: cross-cultural relationship building for mining and resource industries. Based on their decades of experience working at the frontier of Indigenous and non-Indigenous perspectives—First Nation and colonial—they present a rich tapestry of much-needed practical and thoughtful insights to serve as a guide through what has sometimes been a tragic divide. Fairness, respect, and integrity. Words we hear but don't know how to achieve in the confusion of business pressure and social resistance. This is the maze that McPhie and Smith negotiate—with sensitivity and wisdom."

R. ANTHONY HODGE, PhD, P.Eng., Kinross professor of Mining and Sustainability, Queen's University; adjunct professor, Sustainable Minerals Institute, University of Queensland; former CEO, International Council of Mining and Metals

"In the era of economic reconciliation with Indigenous People of Canada, this book is compelling as it relates to how to do business properly with Indigenous nations. It is a must-read if you want to get right and do right by Indigenous People of Canada."

KAREN OGEN-TOEWS, councillor, Wet'suwet'en First Nation; CEO, First Nations LNG Alliance

"This is a timely, provocative, and necessary book. Much of corporate Canada continues to struggle to deeply understand, let alone design and walk the path, to true economic reconciliation with Indigenous Peoples. This book will help build awareness and understanding and challenge long-held myths and biases. The case studies are brief yet illustrative and offer handrails for building relationships with Indigenous communities grounded in trust and shared values and prosperity. Thank you for sharing it with us."

SUSANNAH PIERCE, country chair and GM, Renewables & Energy Solutions, Shell Canada

"*Weaving Two Worlds* is a must-read for anyone involved in the resource economy, Indigenous business, or simply a curious Canadian interested in knowing more on Indigenous business and the resource sector. Both Christy Smith and Mike McPhie are leaders in their field. Thank you for taking the time to write and distribute this important work."

PAUL GRUNER, CEO, Tahltan Nation Development Corporation (TNDC)

"*Weaving Two Worlds* is a timely and insightful read for those in the C-Suite and throughout the corporate engagement platform. Christy Smith and Mike McPhie are knowledgeable experts who bring extensive experience in understanding that committed corporate resource leadership in allyship with Indigenous partners can achieve beneficial Indigenomic outcomes."

ROBERT QUARTERMAIN, P.Geo., DSc

"Christy and Mike have presented the situation through two very different realities, and I think there is something here for all to learn and reflect upon. It is a call to arms in a time when doing 'something' is crucially important...This book presents a cautious but optimistic case for how to proceed from this being the first day of the rest of our lives."

SEAN ROOSEN, chair, board of directors, and CEO, Osisko Development Corporation

"McPhie and Smith provide today's mining CEO with a knowledge- and experience-based multifaceted approach to conducting successful dialogue with First Nation communities. Their methodology focuses on understanding, recognition, and mutual respect combined with transparency and honesty to successfully unravel some of the intricate complexities of engaging with Indigenous Peoples."

TERRY HARBORT, president and CEO, Talisker Resources Ltd.

"Cast away your fragility, take the time to self-reflect, be humble and open to understanding. Let this book be your guide to becoming a leader of the positive changes we all know deep down are needed to build a truly sustainable and inclusive natural resource industry."

DR. FLETCHER MORGAN, president, CEO, and director, TDG Gold Ltd.

"At a time when we need to rethink the natural resource sector as a critical asset in the energy transition, McPhie and Smith open themselves and the sector up to a new, needed approach, one that starts with understanding and reconciliation. It's a roadmap for unlocking new relationships and resources."

STEPHEN D'ESPOSITO, president and CEO, Resolve

"*Weaving Two Worlds* is an excellent, well-presented natural resource development guide that can apply to any sector. In revealing their own roots and life experiences, the authors describe how through a process of self-reflection, understanding, respect, and true reconciliation, it is possible to move forward in a much more equitable and just world together."

MICHAEL MCGEE, Ec.D.(F), MBA, CAFM, PAED, CAPA, economic development coordinator, Bridge River Indian Band (Xwísten)

"*Weaving Two Worlds* takes us on a journey to question ourselves, look at the past, and understand the keys to sincere and respectful engagement with Indigenous communities. A great and powerful book written by two experienced and knowledgeable experts who truly believe in the mutual benefits of reconciliation between the Indigenous Peoples and the resource sector."

FRANÇOIS VÉZINA, senior vice president, Osisko Development Corporation

WEAVING
TWO
WORLDS

CHRISTY SMITH | MICHAEL MCPHIE

WEAVING TWO WORLDS

Economic Reconciliation Between Indigenous Peoples and the Resource Sector

PAGE TWO

Cataloguing in publication information is
available from Library and Archives Canada.
ISBN 978-1-77458-264-0 (paperback)
ISBN 978-1-77458-242-8 (ebook)

Page Two
pagetwo.com

Edited by Amanda Lewis
Copyedited by Christine Lyseng Savage
Cover design by Cameron McKague
Cover illustration by Nahanee Creative
Interior design by Fiona Lee

falkirk.ca

We dedicate this book to you, the reader.
May you place your feet on the ground,
open your heart, listen with intention, and do
something to make our world a better place.

Contents

• Introduction 1

1 **Self-Reflection** 23

2 **Educate Yourself** 45

3 **Consultation Is a Legal Requirement** 65

4 **Land, Water, and Seven Generations** 79

5 **How to Engage** 93

6 **Agreements: How, When, and Why** 113

7 **Allyship and the Opportunity
of Indigenomics** 131

• Acknowledgements 163

• Notes 165

Introduction

IN A recent article in *Maclean's* magazine, Murray Sinclair, a retired senator and former chair of the Canadian Truth and Reconciliation Commission, was asked his thoughts on reconciliation and "shallow symbolic acts," like social media posts and wearing orange T-shirts, versus doing things that are more substantive and could make a tangible difference. It is an important question and one that many may struggle with when seeing injustice, racism, or harm in the world and want to try and do something about it. What is the right response? And what if your response only appears symbolic to some but means something to you? Does that make it wrong or somehow not enough?

Senator Sinclair, with reference to commission member Marie Wilson, responded that what is important is that you "do something"—whatever that is. Whether it's wearing an orange shirt or talking to kids or sending money to a good Indigenous cause, you are doing *something*, and those things are all good.[1]

This book, these stories, and the collaboration of two voices, of two worlds—Indigenous and non-Indigenous—presenting different ways of knowing and understanding is our attempt to try and do something. We do not know if this will change anything or anyone, but we sincerely hope it will. We come to this with humility and recognition that ours are only two voices among many, and we cannot profess to speak for anyone but ourselves.

In sharing the knowledge, experience, and wisdom we have gained over our lives and careers at the front line of relationships between resource companies and Indigenous communities, our hope is that we can help bridge understanding between these two worlds.

Ally and Allyship

Our overarching goal of this work is to shift the thinking of those in the resource sector to seeing themselves as allies with Indigenous communities—recognizing that through deepening understanding, it will be possible to strengthen relationships and create opportunities for both Indigenous and non-Indigenous businesses and communities.

What do we mean by "ally," and what is allyship? *Merriam-Webster* dictionary defines the verb "ally" as to "combine or unite a resource or commodity with (another) for mutual benefit." This has further evolved to the noun "allyship," which refers to "a supportive association with another person or group."

This concept has been further described through Sheree Atcheson's research into diversity in the workplace, where she describes allyship as:

- A lifelong process of building relationships based on trust, consistency, and accountability with marginalized individuals and/or groups of people.

- Not self-defined—work and efforts must be recognized by those you are seeking to ally with.

- An opportunity to grow and learn about ourselves whilst building confidence in others.

In this book, when we refer to being an ally and to allyship, we are referring to the ideas reflected in the above definitions. Also, in being an ally with Indigenous communities:

- The resource sector will be in a supportive association with Indigenous communities.

- The association of the resource sector is recognized and welcomed by the Indigenous community in question.

- There is a recognition that building supportive relationships should be approached as a lifelong effort based on trust, consistency, and accountability.

- Being an ally does not in any way take away an Indigenous community's right or obligation to pursue a just and prosperous future for themselves based on their own terms, defined by them and only them.

Who Is This Book For?

We recognize that there is a diverse and varied level of awareness, understanding, and recognition of the importance of positive relationships between the resource sector and Indigenous Peoples in Canada and globally—and that people come into this discussion with their own history, experiences, and filters through which they see the world. Although we believe this is one of the most critical issues facing the future of both Indigenous communities and the resource sector globally, not everyone shares that view. There are those within the resource sector who are already making positive changes and influencing attitudes within their organizations, their industries, and their families, as well as with friends and others. These are the people who make reconciliation a part of their daily lives, are culturally aware and self-aware, and look for opportunities to move the dialogue forward in a positive way.

There are also those who are aware of and care about the issues, and when confronted with the harsh side of colonialism, they recognize injustice and harm and want to know more. However, they might struggle with understanding Indigenous culture and are not sure how to act or make a difference. They can be challenged by complex legal positions regarding who owns what and how that might affect their own business or personal interests. They might worry about making mistakes in what they say or do, and they may not recognize their own biases. They have heard about white privilege, and they support the ideas of reconciliation, decolonization, and the rights of Indigenous Peoples, but they do not fully understand how they or their organization might engage with these seemingly complex topics. They want to be and to be seen as leaders in working with Indigenous communities. They recognize the importance of this work in the context of the resource sector and are willing to try and learn new ways of doing things. But again, they might struggle with how best to go about doing this.

Is this you?

Are you looking for tools, understanding, and insights into how to engage and build meaningful, respectful relationships with Indigenous Peoples and communities? Are you interested in helping improve the relationship between the resource sector and Indigenous communities?

If so, then this book is for you.

Whether you are a resource company CEO, board member, or manager working with a service or supply company to the resource sector or a future leader in the industry, we believe there is something here for you to learn. Or if you are an individual looking at a possible career in this important sector of the global economy—we think there is something here for you.

We believe that the resource sector and the people within it have a meaningful role to play in advancing reconciliation. We have seen the positive influence when those in positions of power use it to ally themselves with advancing the well-being of Indigenous Peoples, and that is what we are trying to do here—help the resource sector and the people within it to become allies with Indigenous Peoples and provide guidance on how to use their positions of influence, be they big or small, to make true reconciliation possible.

Just because you want to be an ally doesn't mean you will not cause unintentional harm. In your eagerness to do the right thing or to become an ally, you might exhibit guilt, white privilege, or microaggressions, and you might also hold untrue assumptions and stereotypes.

We believe that Indigenous communities can benefit from the support and allyship of the resource sector and the people within it. Whether considering economic prosperity, acknowledgement of the rights of Indigenous Peoples and communities in participating directly in decisions that affect them, or in the ownership of land and resources—and self-determination and pursuits determined solely by the Indigenous community—the resource sector can and should be allies in these pursuits. If this is done right, the outcome will be greater social, environmental, and economic well-being for all.

Of course, much work remains to be done. Insincerity, ignorance, racism, and an absence of respect still exists. Too many leaders in industry have not taken the time to understand the issues, and instead they continue to perpetuate stereotypes. This will continue to be a challenge, and we are not naive enough to think differently. This is the beginning of change, and there is an opportunity to move things forward in a good way. That is the path we are trying to carve and that we hope you will follow.

Economic Reconciliation

So, what is it that we mean when we discuss the idea of economic reconciliation between the resource sector and Indigenous Peoples? Let's start first with reconciliation in the context of Indigenous Peoples, both in Canada and globally. For us, the definition of reconciliation as defined by the Canadian Truth and Reconciliation Commission (TRC) in their 2015 final report captures this the best: "Reconciliation is about establishing and maintaining a mutually respectful relationship between Aboriginal and non-Aboriginal peoples in this country. In order for that to happen, there has to be awareness of the past, acknowledgement of the harm that has been inflicted, atonement for the causes, and action to change behaviour."

As with the negative consequences of such policies as the residential school system, there has been similar harm inflicted on Indigenous Peoples worldwide from the exploitation of natural resources—without, in many cases, any material benefits coming back to them. And these have often been the same people who endured the most harm through environmental destruction, loss of livelihood, cultural and community displacement, and the legacies of scarred landscapes or waterways. Basically, they were enduring all the risk and harm and receiving none of the benefits.

Economic reconciliation is about acknowledging this past and the harm that has come from it, atoning for the causes, and taking concrete steps to change behaviour. This includes such key issues as full recognition of Indigenous rights, prior and informed consent, collaborative/shared decision-making, sharing of benefits, and equity participation.

So, Who Are We?

Christy Smith

My full name is Christina Marie Smith (née White and now Hadath). My maternal great-grandmother is the late Henriette Marie Daniels (Addie) from Cowichan Tribes, and my maternal great-grandfather is the late Ernest Hardy from K'ómoks. Both survivors of the Kuper Island Indian Residential School, they married in 1935. My paternal grandmother, Constance Hardy, also a survivor of the Kuper Island Indian Residential School, married my grandfather, Roy Farrell, of settler descent, in 1956. My biological parents are Diana and Mark Farrell, and my adoptive parents who raised me are Dan and Val White. My Indigenous family is from the Bear clan.

You may have heard others identify themselves in this way. Why do I introduce myself this way? I was taught that it is important to introduce ourselves by first identifying who and where we came from and then to call upon our ancestors and those still with us—by saying their names out loud—to stand by us when we share moments and stories. And they, in essence, share their stories through me.

As noted above, like many of my Indigenous colleagues in my age group, I did not grow up in my community; I was adopted into a white settler home. However, I view myself as lucky and privileged; my adoptive family was loving and let me know when I was really young that I was adopted and from an Indigenous community. Because adoptions were closed back then, they couldn't tell me which community I was from, but in an effort to keep me engaged with wanting to seek my complete identity, they provided me with Indigenous-looking dolls, books, beaded necklaces, and moccasins. In no way did they understand or think about the stereotypes or assumptions associated with these gifts; they did this out of kindness and love and to remind me that I was special. From a young age, my passion was to find my culture, traditions, and ways of knowing, and my ancestral DNA and the Creator pushed me in the direction to find it.

When I went to elementary school, there were a few of us who were Indigenous, but when we were that age, we never cared about race or colour. In Grade 4, my parents asked if I wanted a sister. Well, what kid doesn't want a sibling, especially a sister who could help me combat my two brothers who always banded together against me? I remember that my parents brought out these green hardcover books, and we opened them together. Inside were pictures of Indigenous children; some were on their own and others were in groups of two to five. I remember thinking that some were darker than me, some were lighter; I wondered if maybe one was my cousin or relative. My parents chose to meet a young girl named Jaimie from Nisga'a, who later became my sister. She lived with us from the age of ten until she ran away at age fifteen. Her story is for another book, as it is filled with sadness and the common horrific stories we hear about East Vancouver, including her barely escaping being a victim of Robert Pickton. I visited her multiple times, and I think that was a turning point for me and a realization that I needed to do something to help our people.

After high school I became pregnant with my oldest son, Josh, a.k.a. Ari James; he was my rock and my reason for leaving the party scene and starting to fight for Indigenous rights. At the same time, I met my biological parents and did a personal journey back to K'ómoks to meet family. I remember saying I was going to university, and I was told that I was going to a white man's school to lose who I was. That comment stuck with me. *How could this be*, I wondered, *when I was on a journey to find myself?* At nineteen, I had no idea who I was— regardless of finding my Indigenous way. Now, reflecting back, I see that this was definitely my relatives' reaction to having residential schooling imposed on them.

I decided to move to Edmonton and attend the University of Alberta to obtain my Native Studies degree, as I wanted to become a lawyer and fight for our communities' land to be returned, which in turn would bring healing to our communities and people. Everywhere I went, I immersed myself in Indigenous communities, language, and culture. I learned how to speak Cree, spent time on the Enoch reserve, and participated in sweats and events. I graduated in 2002.

During my years in university, I watched how the Indigenous communities in Alberta tried to get involved in the massive oil and gas spike by positioning themselves to either play an economic role or fight against the industry. What I noticed, and what stood out the most, was that many communities had limited capacity to become business partners—but those who could participate were able to integrate their practices and also provide back to the communities, which in turn supported social programs, daycares, and health care. *Indigenous communities* should *profit from extractive industries—this is bullshit!* kept running through my head. So I spent a year working with non-profits fighting for that right, and then I realized that we hadn't gotten anywhere.

It wasn't until I decided to work for these extractive industries in a management capacity that I could implement change. I'm not going to lie—I was a token "Indian" many times. In

2008 my husband (at the time) and I moved to Fort St. James, and I started working with Terrane Metals at the Mount Milligan Project, which was later sold to Thompson Creek Metals. During this time, in order to combat the tokenism and increase my skills and my language in the business world, I enrolled in my MBA and graduated in 2010. Who was going to mess with an educated Indigenous woman, right?

Over the next five years, I worked for Thompson Creek and then Taseko Mines with the intention of trying to educate the internal management and the C-suite. Did I make a difference? I hoped so, but some days I had my doubts. In 2015, I met Mike McPhie, and we began to collaborate on how to work together to make a difference and strive to overcome the challenges that we both saw in the industry. This is when I became a consultant, and I only worked with clients who were in those two categories that we described at the beginning of this book: those who were already making positive changes and those who wanted to but didn't know how. I have no time for clients who just want to check a box.

Today, I am living and working from the traditional territory of K'ómoks (tuwa akʷs χoχoɫ ʔa xʷ yiχmɛtɛt (ʔa) kʷʊms hɛhaw tʊms gỹɛ)—caretakers of the "land of plenty" since time immemorial (ʔayʾajủʊθəm [eye-uhh-juu-eth-em Island Comox]). I made the journey to a place that feels like home, and I know my ancestors are proud that I speak loudly for them and others in this industry.

Michael McPhie

I am a fourth-generation British Columbian of Scottish and English descent. My great-grandfather on my mom's side came to British Columbia in the early 1900s from Minnesota in search of trees to cut down. With his sons, one of them my grandfather, he built a meaningful forestry and sawmill business in the province that was ultimately purchased by the

American forestry giant, Weyerhaeuser. My dad came from Falkirk, Scotland, in the 1960s, joined the Canadian Armed Forces, and was trained as a medical doctor at Queen's University. My brother and I grew up on the edge of what is now known as the Salish Sea, which joins with the Pacific Ocean on the west coast of Canada. Ours was a typically suburban upbringing in one of the world's more beautiful places. Vancouver is a relatively young city, and it was smaller back then, with its mix of anglophones, immigrants, and Indigenous Peoples. As a child, you only really have a passing awareness of what groups make up a community. I do know that in my early school days, it was mostly white kids, with some Asian and a few Indigenous kids. And I honestly never gave those facts much thought.

I have never experienced racism or prejudice because of my race or where I come from. I am a white middle-class guy, and I know I am lucky to have had the opportunities that I have. I've had to work hard to achieve success, but I know that my path to getting there was easy in comparison to many others. I feel conflicted when I consider that reality—first, because I think the barriers that exist for Indigenous Peoples and other minorities are unfair, and second, because I sometimes feel powerless to influence real change. That is not a great place to be for someone who wants to make things happen and has a strong sense of justice. Which I have.

But as Senator Sinclair said, what is necessary is to start by just doing *something*, and that is what I have been trying to do from the start.

My mom is an educator, and early in her career she was responsible for the First Nations education program for the District of North Vancouver. I remember hearing many stories of her work, including the building of a longhouse with the Squamish First Nation, which is still to this day used for teaching young people in the region about the Indigenous culture and traditions of the Squamish and Coast Salish people.

As a family we travelled by sailboat around the coast of BC in summers and found ourselves visiting many of the First Nations communities that are dotted throughout the Pacific Northwest. We passed through like so many others, seeing evidence of once-vibrant cultures with magnificent totem poles and longhouses surrounded by rundown homes and vehicles and equipment lying rusted in fields. There was often a feeling of decay in the air, seeing only a few people, and dogs walking the streets in search of their next meal.

I learned that these were reserves designated by the Government of Canada many decades earlier. A reserve—or "rez," as it was referred to by some—was a place where people who were once free to move, guided by the seasons, food, and their traditional territories, were forced to live. A place that, through colonization and government policy, had a small fraction of what it used to have.

I had no real understanding of colonial history or the subjugation of Indigenous Peoples in Canada, much of which still exists to this day. I did not know about residential schools or the Sixties Scoop when, under the direction of the Government of Canada, the national police force, the RCMP, forcibly removed children from their homes and took them away. With many never to return.

But I could see that what was on the reserves was not the same as what was in the surrounding non-Indigenous communities. What I recall feeling was confusion. How could anyone who walks into a traditional longhouse of the Coast Salish not be impressed? Or see the art and the clothes and learn about the proud history and traditions of First Peoples and not think it is amazing?

But then we would see the conditions on some reserves and hear stories about substance abuse and social despair within some First Nations communities, and we learned that things, for many, were not good. Being an educator and working with youth, my mom always seemed to have a sense of optimism about the future. This, I think, was because of the energy and leadership potential she would see in the young people she was teaching. Things were hard, yes. But progress was being made then, and we are seeing the results of that now. I think I was still too young to understand what was going on. But those early experiences established in me an awareness of injustice, a desire to understand more, and some recognition that there was much more to this story and our history than we were being exposed to through traditional channels.

Fast-forward twenty years, and I found myself with a science degree and working in the mining industry in the Arctic. Looking for diamonds. Which we found quite a lot of. It was there that I was introduced to the Inuit people of northern Canada—and to barren ground caribou, muskox, the many different words used to describe snow and ice, northern lights, cold beyond anything I even knew was possible, and traditional ecological knowledge. I also became aware, through the permitting and ultimate development of Canada's first diamond mine, Ekati (and other mining projects in the north), of the often-challenged relationship between Indigenous Peoples in the north and the mining industry.

Since then and over the past years, I have been fortunate to serve at almost every level within industry and, for a short time, with government, advancing projects and public policy. I have done this throughout Canada and globally as a CEO, a chair of the board, and a senior advisor. I have raised hundreds of millions of dollars, taken companies public on the Toronto Stock Exchange, and led the development efforts of major projects in several different countries. I have seen and been a part of some real success stories, and I have also seen more than one project, initiative, or government policy decision go sideways for many different reasons. I have seen that success, or lack thereof, always comes down to people and how they are treated and involved in decisions that affect them.

To exist, the resource sector relies on access to land and water and the valuable things that exist or grow and live in these areas. Indigenous Peoples across the globe have been the stewards of these same lands and resources for thousands of years. And, despite the disruptions associated with colonization in Canada and many parts of the world, the rights of those same people have never been extinguished and are now rightly being recognized once again by the courts, governments, and institutions that make up civil society. I see that as just, but it has taken far too long to be recognized. The fact that it is now, though, is reason for hope and optimism. That is where I come from in this discussion.

How Industry Got Here

Conflict around major resource projects is nothing new. In fact, it has been a factor to a greater or lesser degree in almost all major projects that involve altering the landscape or waterways or infringe on private property, culture, or the well-being of communities.

The reasons for that conflict have evolved over time as our collective awareness of the fragility of the natural environment and ecosystems is better understood, human populations have exploded, economies and societies have modernized, and values have changed. What has not changed, though, is our need for the products and services that come from these projects and industries. Minerals, metals, wood products, and energy are critical parts of every aspect of our modern life, and that is only set to increase in the future.

Industry practices have changed, in the most part for the better, in step with this evolution. And we have come a long way since the attitudes of the past, which can be epitomized by the likes of "Flying Phil" Gaglardi, the former mayor of Kamloops and the BC minister of public works under Premier W.A.C. Bennett, who said that "air pollution is the smell of money." For many, though, that change has not happened quickly or materially enough, and much remains to be done.

Before we consider the issue of the future of relationships between the resource sector and Indigenous Peoples, it is helpful to consider how the attitudes of and toward industry got to where they are today. We also need to look at how society's perspective of industry has been shaped by events and practices of the past and why it is hard to move beyond that when, in some cases, the consequences of those are still with us.

Marshall McLuhan once said, "The new is always made up of the old, or rather, what people see in the new is always the old thing. The rear-view mirror." Many see their lives and events happening in the world through that perspective—seeing what is happening today through the lens of what they think may have been great about the past, while often ignoring those things that were not. Or vice versa. Our realities today are shaped by those experiences we have had, and we can only really move forward if we acknowledge where we have come from and recognize both the good and the bad of the past.

So, before thinking of the future and where to go from here, let us consider our past in the context of how industrial development was done back in the "good old days" and how that might be influencing perspectives today.

Romanticizing Our Industrial Past

For many who make their living in the resource sector or who are of an older generation, there is a tendency to romanticize the past and immortalize the pioneers and builders of our primary industries. They see them as providing a foundation for our modern economy and allowing all of us the opportunity to have the quality of life many of us enjoy today. And from that perspective, they are right, whether we are talking about the national railways that link the east and west of North America, the electrical infrastructure that delivers inexpensive power to millions, or the major roads and ports that enable global trade. Much of this was built decades ago, and almost all of it before modern environmental protection considerations, let alone consideration of the rights of Indigenous Peoples.

It is common to celebrate the explorers, political leaders, and industrialists who "opened up" new areas to development and championed infrastructure and resource development. For example, former BC Premier W.A.C. Bennett was featured on the cover of *Time* magazine in 1966 and applauded throughout North America and globally for his drive to construct hydroelectric dams, cut trees, and build metal and coal mines throughout Canada's most western province. To this day, he is immortalized by many as a builder who was part of the good old days when we could "get things done!"

US President Franklin D. Roosevelt's New Deal, which was designed to kick-start the American economy post-Depression, was widely celebrated for its massive infrastructure build throughout the country. In this deal, nearly every river with adequate flow was dammed for electricity by the Army Corps of Engineers. This included the construction of the iconic Hoover Dam, which many credit as being one of the keys to increasing the industrial capacity of America, allowing the country to build more tanks, airplanes, and ships than the Germans and to ultimately be one of the key factors in winning the Second World War.

And let us not forget George Stephen, the Scottish-born engineer who led the building of the Canadian Pacific Railway, which connected the east and west coast of one of the world's largest countries in the late nineteenth century.

Along with these are smaller but locally or regionally important mining, forestry, and energy projects, many of which were built by people—almost all men—with a pioneering spirit and a "get it done" attitude. We can see that history throughout Canada, North America, and globally in major projects that continue to this day, and in the many ghost towns and abandoned industrial sites that dot the global landscape.

Another Side to This Story

The legacy of all these projects is significant. They have provided access to inexpensive electricity and the ability to efficiently transport goods, and they have played a major part in creating the modern conveniences, economies, and societies of today. However, there is another side to many of these projects that involves the profound social and environmental impacts that came as a result. In some cases, those legacies continue to be experienced by communities or are evident in the state of the natural environment where they took place.

For example, an achievement often referred to in the context of Premier Bennett was the building of the iconic W.A.C. Bennett Dam in northern BC. This immense infrastructure investment, completed in 1968, had the floodwaters of ten rivers and creeks converge into a massive hydroelectric project to form the Williston Reservoir. This one power project provides 25 percent of Canada's westernmost province's electricity needs today, and at the time it had the largest generating station in the world.

However, in this case local First Nations were not even informed, much less consulted, about the project, and much of their traditional lands were lost forever. The new reservoir resulted in the flooding of some 350,000 acres of land, with little regard to the environmental or social consequences that resulted. In 2016, almost fifty years later, the provincial utility, BC Hydro, apologized for the "profound and painful" impact on First Nations and the environment from this development.

With the major buildup of power infrastructure under Roosevelt in America, the impact on rivers and fish populations is likely almost incalculable. Many studies have weighed the impacts on the environment and people from the damming of US rivers such as the Columbia and the Rio Grande, and many of the dams that were put in then are now being removed. The Hoover Dam is truly a remarkable feat of engineering, even to this day. However, it does not take long in looking at the history to discover the displacement and impact to the Native American tribes of the region or the immense loss of life in the workers who constructed it, due to the extreme heat and unsafe working conditions.

The celebrated building of Canada's national railroad is another example. Linking one coast to the other over thousands of kilometres and helping form the union of this massive country is a huge engineering achievement. However, one part of the dark side of this history relates to the use of more than fifteen thousand Chinese labourers, who were brought in during the 1880s, to do the most dangerous and difficult work. It is said that one worker died for every mile of track laid through the Rocky Mountains between Calgary and Vancouver.

There are numerous stories like these that span every major industry. Indigenous communities often paid the highest price and received the least in the way of benefit. That is Canada's history, and the history of a significant part of the world.

Raising these issues is not meant to denigrate the importance of these industries to the basic fabric that allows us to enjoy the standard of living most of us have today. It is to point out that the way in which they were undertaken, and how the communities and environment were affected, would not be acceptable by any reasonable standard applied today. Furthermore, we tend to think of these examples of things that happened far in the past, whereas we continue to encounter major environmental and social challenges associated with industrial development in many parts of the world today.

The adage that past behaviour is a good predictor of the future if the same people are involved applies. And it is in this context and reality that those involved in industry must face when we enter communities to promote the next major project. It is not enough to say we have the best engineers and scientists involved. That has not always worked, as we have seen.

Where We Are Now

The resource sector both here in Canada and globally remains a major part of the economy and global supply chain. Recent statistics published by the United Nations Environment Program (UNEP) International Resource Panel showed that with the rapid rise of population and per capita income, the twentieth century witnessed growth in annual extraction of construction materials by a factor of 34, of ores and minerals by 27, of fossil fuels by 12, of biomass by 3.6, and of total material extraction by 8. The material footprint per capita has also increased at a significant rate, according to statistics released by the UN recently. In 1990, about 8.1 metric tons of natural resources were used to satisfy an individual's needs. In 2017, that rose to 12.2 metric tons, an increase of 50 percent.[2] More simply, this means that each of us use over twelve thousand kilograms of resources every year to live, with those in rich countries having the most voracious appetite.

There are, of course, wide variations both between and within countries in this. But what these statistics demonstrate is that our dependence on natural resources for the functioning of our modern economy and society remains, and it will continue to well into the future. It also means that we are likely to see more conflict over projects that are proposed in areas that are deemed environmentally sensitive, or that are considered spiritual or subject to unresolved Indigenous claims or interests, or where they encounter resistance from communities and government.

Ultimately, concerns from the public are reflected in government policy that could, if not adequately addressed, impact the viability of entire industries. Whether we are talking about pipelines, mines, oil and gas projects, forestry, fisheries, or infrastructure, hard questions are being asked, and industry is being forced to respond.

The questioning and advocacy against certain parts of the resource industry is also being reflected in investment decisions by major sources of capital. Pension funds, for example, which reached a staggering value of USD$35 trillion at the end of 2020,[3] are under increasing pressure from their constituencies to assess where they direct their investments. With the environment and social governance (ESG) issues playing an increasingly important part in the evaluation of whether specific investments meet the necessary criteria to be approved, the entire resource sector is put under a lot of pressure, and, in some cases, threatens the viability of entire parts of it.

The transition from the approach of the last century's builders to today's industry leaders being allied with Indigenous communities and stewards of the environment will be key to success in the future. We recognize that the path to a more sustainable future with regard to economic reconciliation with Indigenous Peoples is not a straight one, and there remain major issues to address. Conflicts continue around projects. Communities are not being engaged with to anywhere near the degree they should be, and in many cases the rights of Indigenous Peoples are not being respected. Tailings dams continue to fail. In places like the Amazon, forest ecosystems are being ravaged by industry that's enabled by lax government policy. Rivers and oceans continue to suffer under the pressure of unchecked development, and our global climate continues to warm. And the true commitment of management, boards, and governments to doing the right thing varies widely.

Industry has improved in many ways, though; there is no doubt about that. And, we would argue, many are moving it in the right direction. But just as many remain at odds with true sustainability, and recognizing and acknowledging past failures and the reasons for them is essential in being able to move forward.

1

Self-Reflection

WE ARE starting this discussion with an examination of what we believe to be one of the single most important parts of this work, which is looking at who you are, what you believe, and what you know and may not know. Because in considering building resilient relationships with others, the first step is to "know thyself."

Self-examination is not something most of us are very good at. It is easier to attribute issues and problems to others rather than to take ownership of them yourself.

What is critical in the work we are discussing here is to recognize what biases you might carry with you into a new relationship. To recognize how you might come across to others. To ask yourself whether you are aware of the history of colonialism and subjugation of Indigenous Peoples in Canada and globally. And to think about how you actually feel when you hear about that history. Does it make you feel ashamed of our governments and leaders for the way in which they treated Indigenous Peoples? Or do you feel something else? When you see symbols of Indigenous spirituality and culture, do you feel curious, or do you feel threatened or offended somehow?

It is important to learn to recognize how, as a non-Indigenous person, you might see Indigenous Peoples as either valued potential partners or as likely barriers to your business pursuits. Also, learn to reflect on how you react and feel when you learn about the tragic stories of children as young as three years old dying in residential schools in Canada over the past one-hundred-plus years. If you were an industry executive responsible for shareholders' money, would you consider your understanding and relationship with Indigenous Peoples to be a primary focus for the company or just something grouped in with other ESG (environmental, social, and corporate governance) initiatives to provide the appearance of caring?

Think honestly about whether you truly believe qualified Indigenous Peoples should be at the highest levels of industry and business management. Or consider how you would feel if your boss and the owner of the company you are with was an Indigenous person. What about an Indigenous woman?

And we could go on with more and more questions like these. There are many. Our point in raising them is that if the overall goal here is to try to turn industry from being an adversary at odds with Indigenous communities to allies—where there is work toward a common purpose and set of values and goals—then right from the beginning, it must be very clear to everyone what baggage, what biases, what stereotypes, and what lack of knowledge and understanding people are coming to the table with. Because without that, it will be next to impossible to develop meaningful, resilient relationships.

The ancient Greek maxim of "know thyself" applies here because knowing your own history and biases will help you recognize how those might be influencing what you experience and the beliefs you hold. In going through this chapter, think about these questions and subjects. Think about your own experiences and the beliefs you might have. This is not supposed to be easy. And we expect that if you do this assessment honestly, it will make you uncomfortable at times. But it is in this place of discomfort where real learning and a deeper level of understanding begins.

Starting Point

In Canada and other countries, colonialism is best understood as Indigenous Peoples' forced disconnection from their land, culture, and communities by another group. It has historical connotations, but it needs to be recognized as continuing today. Colonial practices and policies are systemic—they remain evident in law, legislation, health care, government, social services, policing, education, and how natural resources are accessed.

In the context of resources, the most important element of colonialism today is the loss of land and access to it. Canada uses words like "progress" and "development" to allow the theft of traditional territories to continue. The unequal power relation is perpetuated, as Indigenous Peoples are not consulted on matters that relate directly to their people and lands.

As noted by the distinguished professor and author Robin Wall Kimmerer in her book *Braiding Sweetgrass*, "In the settler mind, land was property, real estate, capital, or natural resources. But to our people, it was everything: identity, the connection to our ancestors, the home of our nonhuman kinfolk, our pharmacy, our library, the source of all that sustained us."

The whole point of this chapter is to have you do your own self-reflection. Awareness is the foundation of developing good relationships and understanding decolonization. It is okay if you do identify that you are bringing assumptions to the table; this is about education and reframing how we engage. This book was not written to make you feel bad or guilty; it was written to develop and encourage understanding. The assumptions, stereotypes, perceptions, and comparisons of one race or person to another are major barriers to the development of authentic relationships. We often do this without knowing the impact it can have on the development of true relationships.

It is important to recognize the place where you are coming from when engaging with Indigenous Peoples. This chapter will be exploring privilege, white fragility, guilt, assumptions, and stereotypes, while also encouraging self-reflection and introspection.

When you are engaging, ask yourself some questions, such as:

- Are you coming from a place of privilege?

- Are you coming from a place of white fragility?

- Are you coming from a place of guilt?

- Are you coming from a place of assumptions and stereotypes?

- What unconscious assumptions and beliefs are you carrying with you, and how do they affect your understanding of Indigenous Peoples and situations?

These questions may be cause for surprise and serious reflection. Be prepared to feel defensive and for uncomfortable feelings to arise. This reflection will be different for everyone.

CHRISTY: As an Indigenous woman who has been gifted with this understanding, as good practice, I ask myself on a regular basis when I engage with anyone (even friends and colleagues) if I am coming to this relationship from a place of privilege. Am I perceiving myself as more knowledgeable, or as coming from a place of higher status? This constant self-check allows me to be humble and truly have valuable interactions.

I have been advocating on a regular basis for this type of self-reflection training to be provided to non-Indigenous people who are working with Indigenous groups. This training was recently suggested to a local government that has been sitting at the table with an Indigenous government. The point of the table is to work in collaboration, but the reality is that there are many members coming from a place of privilege, a place of "I went to school for this, and science says this." Discounting Indigenous knowledge or suggesting that colonial teachings are better than Indigenous knowledge and ways of knowing has created frustration and distrust in the relationship. When self-reflection training was suggested, there was apprehension and frustration on the colonial government side: "Why do we need to take this training? We already know what we are doing." This question and comment made it very clear that self-reflection and decolonization training was very much needed. Privilege and white fragility were breaking down the relationship.

MIKE: As a middle-class Canadian man who has never experienced racism and has never been "looked over" for a position because of my gender or background, I come to this discussion with humility, respect for others who have had to endure a lot more than me, and some wisdom from what I have learned throughout my life and career.

I believe that beginning with our own self-reflection is critical before we dive into a deeper discussion on Indigenous issues and the resource sector. This is something we should all do more of, and it is the essential place to start. Understanding ourselves will allow us to be fully present in a discussion about relationship building and reconciliation.

Let's now look at the major topics that require reflection and consideration in the dialogue between Indigenous and non-Indigenous people.

Privilege

There is hardly a penalty for lack of awareness and education for people who belong to the dominant group in society;
however, the way this lack of awareness and education affects
minority groups can be severe.

Historically, white, male heterosexuals have marginalized
other groups in what is now Canada. They have held the power
and have benefitted disproportionally from those dynamics
in comparison to other members of society. This continues to
be very evident in the C-suite positions in the resource industry today. Examining the dominant membership of resource
company boards today, diversity remains limited. Some leading companies are making diversity and inclusion key to their
board structure going forward, but much work remains to
see true equity at this level of corporate management and
decision-making.

Membership on a corporate board today most likely means
that the person is coming from a place of privilege. In some
cases, it could be a result of generational wealth or contacts
passed down to them, helping to open the door to these positions. In others, these connections come through peer groups
or other valued external relationships.

Do you perceive yourself as better, richer, or more knowledgeable than other people? Have you ever? Have you come to
a relationship with a preconceived notion based on your place
of privilege?

It is important to recognize benefits that you take for
granted as a result of your positionality and place in society. It is
about looking at the advantages you have because of your position, as opposed to the disadvantages minority or oppressed
groups suffer. It is also important to recognize the situations
and positions you are spared from as a result of your privilege.

CHRISTY: I remember a story an elder once told me. His mother had gotten a job at the Hudson's Bay Company, and as a surprise, she bought him a bike. This was the first bike ever to be bought and brought onto the reserve. He was so eager to ride his new bike, and he woke up first thing in the morning, intending to feel the wind on his face and feel freedom. He ran outside and found that his new bike was gone. All day, he caught glimpses of his bike being ridden by other kids. That night it was returned to his yard. This occurred for several weeks until, he told me with a chuckle, he let the air out of the tires one evening. The next morning his bike was there, so he pumped up the tires and rode it from dawn to dusk. He was fine sharing his bike, but he wanted a turn. "It wasn't like it was being stolen," he said, as every night the bike was returned. He recognized his position of privilege, even in an impoverished community, and was never angry about sharing. His wisdom taught me that we can all be privileged in some way, regardless of our position, but how we recognize that privilege and act in regard to that space and place of privilege is so important.

Privilege can include:

- Walking into the drugstore and finding that all the makeup, Band-Aids, and hair products cater to your hair and skin type.

- Seeing mostly people of your race represented on television and in books.

- Being able to move through life without being racially profiled or unfairly stereotyped.

- Never being asked to speak for all the people of your racial group.

White Fragility

You may have stumbled across this term. How do you know if you are you coming from a place of white fragility? Are you going to take offence if you are called out on being white, privileged, and a settler? Or if you are told that you benefit from a systemically racist system?

What is white fragility? White fragility can affect relationships between proponents, non-Indigenous governments, settlers, and Indigenous communities. When you are called out in respect to your privilege or your perceived opinions, this can trigger moral defensiveness: "I am a good person. I am not racist." But what if you are privileged and are experiencing white fragility, and you just have not identified your position in the relationship?

This can be the number one reason a relationship deteriorates. Robin DiAngelo coined the term "white fragility" to describe a defensive reaction by white people when they are questioned in respect to views on race and racism. In her 2018 book, *White Fragility*, she writes, "Whites have not had to build tolerance for racial discomfort and thus when racial discomfort arises, whites typically respond as if something is 'wrong,' and blame the person or event that triggered the discomfort (usually a person of color)."

From Peggy McIntosh's article "White Privilege: Unpacking the Invisible Knapsack" (a famous and foundational article): "I have come to see white privilege as an invisible package of unearned assets that I can count on cashing in each day, but about which I was 'meant' to remain oblivious." Whiteness is viewed as normative and race-less; white people don't have to carry the burden of race or colour. Race is carried by people of colour. White is considered objective. This is evident in media—white people are not labelled, but people of colour are.

What is your instinctive response when an Indigenous community states that you are on their land? I have seen many proponents start arguing that they have the right, via tenures and permits, to be there. This reaction can lead to adversarial relationships, and in a way, it is an attempt to erase the Indigenous community's legitimate right to their land, and their continued existence on it.

Indigenous Peoples have been on the land since time immemorial. Proponents on Indigenous lands are settlers on unceded lands. If you take offence at being called a settler or a temporary visitor, or if you take offence at a perception, you need to reflect on your own white fragility. Feelings of discomfort and white fragility can include anger, shame, withdrawal, guilt, and emotional incapacitation. Those feelings, although legitimate, are not helpful.

Try to *ditch that shit* (your privilege and white fragility) at the door. Start with being humble, and then focus on developing your relationships from a place of integrity.

Fear and Guilt

When you are engaging, are you coming from a place of guilt or a place of fear? Some proponents we have worked with are afraid of engaging with Indigenous nations, as they are scared to say the wrong thing, and they have a fear of offending someone—so much so that they take the shortest path of engagement and only do so to check the proverbial boxes of consultation and engagement. We have heard many times that engaging with Indigenous communities causes delays— that they are adversarial, and that engagement leads to more, unnecessary, work.

However, it should be very clear that although this is rapidly changing, Indigenous communities are also afraid of engaging for several reasons. One is distrust of the colonial permitting process that has been imposed on them and distrust of government in general. This distrust is evident and problematic not only in the resource sector but also in health care, social services, justice, education, and other government services. The resource sector has historically set foot on traditional Indigenous territory, leaving a trail of environmental degradation without care or consideration of Indigenous ways and values.

Another factor is the perception that if Indigenous communities do engage, it may be assumed that this indicates they support the project. This sometimes results in no communication being offered, and it can be a real challenge for proponents. The Indigenous communities' silence is not necessarily opposition; it is a fear that the engagement may somehow be used against them or that it infers consent.

This identifies the challenge of how can we have successful dialogue and open communication when both parties may be coming to the table with apprehension and fear?

We have seen many examples of where discussions with project proponents and government are not being held in a good way from an Indigenous perspective. They are not seen as safe or trauma-free, and that environment can create fear. Proponents and governments who create these environments, whether deliberately or just because they are not aware, are unlikely to have successful engagement in this context. We will discuss this further in Chapter 2.

Another factor to consider in relationships is guilt. Are you engaging and exhibiting guilt for past wrongs? Do you feel somehow responsible?

CHRISTY: I have heard the phrase, "It is so sad what happened to you and your community," and I recommend that you do not use it. We don't want people to pity us. Pity just leads into a colonial loop of denial, where it's thought that these actions were done in the past and couldn't happen today. This is not looking at impacts today—which is what is needed. Understanding history is important, yes, but it is time to focus on the now—reconciliation. You can be sympathetic. Bad things happened; that is true. Recognize them and understand them, but in doing so, be present in the conversation now, and focus on how to make things better in the future.

Stereotypes/Assumptions

CHRISTY: A stereotype is a widely held assumption, image, or concept. It is a shared, generalized idea of something. Sometimes stereotypes can seem positive, but they should be seen as negative, as people are judged based on ideas/norms and not merit. Members of a group lose their individuation as they are generalized. I have many stories about how stereotypes or assumptions have caused problems, made me feel creeped out, or just made me laugh. I have had many experiences where people wanted to touch me, or asked me to do prayers because Indigenous Peoples are stereotyped as being spiritual. I have also had people refuse to offer me an alcoholic beverage because I am Indigenous, perpetuating yet another stereotype.

I have not been impacted by these assumptions as much as I have seen other Indigenous Peoples be impacted by stereotypes that have led to microaggression, then prejudice, and then turned into racism and oppression. I have watched First Nations Peoples in communities who are afraid to seek health care. I have seen the RCMP offer a ride to a First Nations person en route to their reserve but then actually drive them twenty kilometres in the opposite direction. I have heard the fear from elders who are afraid to walk down a road, worried that they may be struck by something being thrown out of a window at them. And I have stories of women who live in constant fear that they may be the next murdered or missing Indigenous woman.

The following are important questions to ask yourself:

- Are you bringing preconceived notions or assumptions to a relationship?

- Are you inadvertently stereotyping people?

- Are there any other assumptions you have that may actually be false?

- How can we change the things we think? How do we combat the perpetuation of these myths and stereotypes?

- What stereotypes are held about Indigenous Peoples?

- Why do these get perpetuated?

When I met my father-in-law, Richard Chandler—who is British born, has a photographic memory, and is super intelligent—he asked me about every myth, stereotype, and assumption that pertains to Indigenous Peoples. I was excited to engage in conversation for hours and days about how these stereotypes and assumptions impact our Indigenous communities daily. When we started talking about Indigenous history, he said something that resonated with me: "Knowledge is powerful; however, a *little* bit of knowledge is dangerous— that is the root of misunderstandings and assumptions. A little bit of knowledge is what causes the problems within our society today."

A huge assumption often held is that all First Nations communities are the same. Pan-Indianism is a good way to get thrown out of a community. Pan (presence across nations)-

Indianism is the assumption that all First Nations are culturally the same, that we hold the same values to a specific area. It is the homogenization of culturally distinct and historically unique communities and peoples. When proponents are engaging, I have noticed there is an assumption that all nations will have the same concerns about projects on their traditional territories. Sure, there are similar concerns among nations, but they all stem from differing connections to and relationships with the land, distinct cultures, and unique perspectives and histories. Some project areas have a variety of nations that have overlapping and shared interests that range from employment to cultural values associated to that particular land base. I have seen proponents assume that if they have one nation in support of a project, all other nations should also be in support. This assumption is very dangerous.

What is important in this is to consider what stereotypes and assumptions you bring into your conversations with Indigenous communities and where those come from. Be curious. Ask questions and do not assume. Humility is a recognition that you do not know everything—and in this area of Indigenous culture and knowledge, it can be guaranteed that you do not.

Unconscious Bias

Unconscious biases are everywhere—from the neighbourhood that we choose to live in to the close friends that we keep and the people we date. Developments in neuroscience now demonstrate that many biases are formed throughout life and held at the subconscious level, mainly through societal and parental conditioning, through nurturing. In other words, these biases are not natural—they are learned. We gather millions of bits of information, and our brains process that information in a certain way, unconsciously categorizing and formatting it into familiar patterns. Though most of us have difficulty accepting or acknowledging it, we all do this. Gender, ethnicity, disability, sexuality, body size, profession, and so on—all of these influence the assessments that we make of people, and they form the basis of our relationships with others and with the world at large.[4]

And we would argue that these same subconscious biases have a profound impact on the perception of Indigenous Peoples in our modern society. We have seen and heard it time and time again—particularly in the context of people who have grown up over the past fifty years and have been exposed to the more common racist and derogatory attitudes toward First Nations and Indigenous Peoples; a constructed bias and continued negative perception of Indigenous Peoples persists today. Or maybe it is just ignorance and lack of exposure to examples of successful Indigenous leaders. Or perhaps bias has been shaped by images in the media of protestors or, in more urban environments, of homelessness and substance abuse.

This is a difficult subject but one that must be addressed head-on before you are able to absorb and learn from what is presented in the remainder of this book. You must examine your subconscious biases.

Consider, both as an individual and as a team member or leader in your organization, what your unconscious biases are when it comes to Indigenous Peoples. And how are those impacting your ability to understand, empathize with, or create deeper relationships with those same people? Further, what is the impact of unconscious bias on the ability of your team or company to advance their understanding and support of issues like reconciliation?

Consider asking some questions, both of yourself and your team, to assess where some of those biases might be. For example, try these ones:

When you see a news report about a First Nations or Indigenous group opposing an industrial project, which of the following reflects how you might think?

- I wonder what is concerning this community to the degree that they would go to the effort of protesting like this? Is it the environment? Their safety? Their way of life? Have their concerns been ignored?

- They are obviously just looking for more money.

- They are just looking for more attention.

- Man, get out of the way and let industry get on with creating jobs.

When you see a person in an urban environment who might appear to be Indigenous and who is in a tough-looking state, possibly under the influence of something and maybe homeless, which of these things might you think?

- I wonder what happened for him to end up in this kind of a situation. Is he a residential school survivor, or was he possibly displaced from his own community for some reason?

- Man, our society is going to hell.

- These freeloaders should just clean themselves up and get jobs.

You have a two o'clock project meeting scheduled with the leadership of an Indigenous community. The timing works out great because you can meet for an hour and then get back to the airport for your five o'clock flight home. Perfect! You show up a few minutes early and are asked to wait in a boardroom for the chief of the community to show up. A half-hour passes and she or he does not show. The band administrator comes in to see you and lets you know that the meeting must be rescheduled, as there was a death in the community and the chief had to comfort the family members. In hearing this news, which of these statements reflects how you might react?

- Immediately understand and respect that, as the elected leader of the community, the chief must attend to a situation like this. That your inconvenience is insignificant in comparison to the needs of their community and that you will just need to come back when it is more appropriate. You also offer any assistance if it could be helpful and thank them for letting you know. You show yourself out and send a message to the chief later, expressing your condolences.

- Become annoyed that you "wasted" this time.

- Think this is just another example of the troubles within Indigenous communities.

- Wonder how Indigenous communities expect to join the modern economy with all of these social challenges.

You are advertising for a senior vice-president for your company, and that person would be responsible for corporate affairs and the environment. They require some technical background in environmental science or engineering and a good understanding of the policies and regulations the company must operate under. Your company has a policy of promoting diversification and building relationships with Indigenous communities. In this situation, which of the following would you be most likely to do?

- Instruct your human resources team to research all avenues to try and attract a diverse set of candidates.

- Look at ways in which to attract strong Indigenous candidates to this position and consider how to frame and adapt the qualifications such that HR has the greatest chance of success in finding qualified candidates.

* Follow the traditional recruitment practice of posting ads stating "diverse candidates encouraged to apply" but limiting efforts to frame the position so that Indigenous candidates are likely to be successful.

* Begin an internal process to identify and support diverse employees with an Indigenous background early in their careers, and support them to be able to pursue executive management positions in the future.

You have a major contract available with one of your projects. Your company has an agreement with an Indigenous community, and you want to encourage economic opportunity for them, but you know that currently they would not be able to successfully bid on this. Which of the following are you most likely to do?

* Contact the economic development officer, make them aware of the opportunity, and indicate that you would like to consider what your company could do to facilitate the community's success in this activity. Together, you then look for creative ways to finance the purchase of equipment and/or training and work to set them up for success.

* Exclude them from the RFP process because you know they cannot compete.

* Send out the RFP and include them so that you meet the obligations of your agreement but know they will not be successful even if they bid.

The examples above are constructed in such a way that it is easy to recognize when negative biases would disadvantage Indigenous Peoples in terms of actions or attitudes. However, it is not always so straightforward, and often biases are more subtle. That does not make them any less important to be aware of, though. As with other marginalized groups in society or in the workplace, biases can have a material impact on how things work and how people are treated.

It is important to be aware of your own biases. This also involves "slowing ourselves down ... and being aware when we're beginning to make stereotypic associations."⁵ If we can do this and undertake our own process of self-reflection, it can be a powerful step forward in creating an environment of awareness and learning—and through this, building the foundation for trust, more meaningful relationships, and reconciliation.

Microaggressions

Microaggressions are somewhat similar to stereotypes, assumptions, and unconscious biases; however, they tend to be unconsciously expressed and less obvious. Microaggressions happen frequently all around us on a daily basis. Microaggressions are the everyday, subtle, intentional—and oftentimes unintentional—interactions or behaviours that communicate some sort of bias toward historically marginalized groups. Over time and through accumulation, they can cause serious harm, including harm to an individual's mental and physical health. Examples of microaggresions can include the following:

- Imitating accents.

- Assuming that people of colour are service workers.

- Commenting on how well an Asian Canadian speaks English, which presumes the Asian Canadian was not born in Canada.

- Asking, "Where are you from?" (assuming that someone not white is foreign-born).

Angela, a woman who Christy had the privilege of mentoring, was chosen to work in Africa on an Indigenous internship program. The trip to Africa was a dream come true, and it was life-changing for Angela. She would FaceTime Christy regularly and tell amazing stories of how they were helping the Indigenous communities in Africa and how the children in the village were her passion and soul. For Angela, being Indigenous herself, this was very important. One particular FaceTime call resonated. She talked about how, when the Canadian representatives came over to Africa to see how the project was going, there was one representative who jerked away when the African children went to touch her, and she carried a very large bottle of sanitizer. To the children—who had nothing and were barely clothed—this government representative was like a famous star or royalty. Physically moving away from people of another race is a form of microaggression. The key in this, as with so much of what we are discussing here, is about awareness and sensitivity about how individual actions, comments, and references can affect someone else. Racism is racism regardless of whether it is intentional or not. "Micro" does not mean small, nor will the impact be if it goes unchecked.

Conclusion

So, how does this make you feel?

How would members of your executive react to the idea of doing an exercise in self-reflection? Would they engage? Would they care? Or would they only participate out of an obligation to the latest company culture efforts of the CEO and human resources department—and then, when they go home and discuss the day with their spouses or partners, disclose that they really thought it was all a bit much?

This is where self-reflection gets real.

What do you really feel? What do you and your team truly believe in? This process will never work unless you are authentic in both who you are and what you believe. Most of us have read corporate social responsibility reports or company statements of how much companies "care" about people. About the environment. About diversity. About their relationships with Indigenous Peoples. But then we witness or read about something quite different in terms of how that same company is carrying out their business. Or we are privy to private conversations between those same executives who signed their names to those aspirational reports or statements and hear how they truly feel about Indigenous Peoples or other marginalized groups.

Both of us have experienced these inconsistencies in different ways—one of us as a highly educated and experienced Indigenous woman in a leadership position who has had to endure racism, sexism, and misogyny in the workplace; the other as a white, professional male who has served at senior levels of corporations and government and who is trying to make positive change but has encountered a lack of knowledge, empathy, and awareness (and, yes, racism) in those environments.

This is not to say that everyone in the resource sector is this way, as that is not in any way the truth. There are some tremendous people who work every day to try and make a difference at all levels within many companies. And nothing we are saying should detract from that work they are doing.

The truth of the matter is, though, the real power in the resource sector—the real money and the real influence—remains in the hands of a relatively small number of people and organizations. Some of those people and organizations are enlightened and, we believe, committed to moving this dialogue forward, making real change, and building good relationships. Embracing real reconciliation. They are self-aware. They have teams that do self-reflection. They believe in a world that is more equitable, fair, and just. And they act accordingly.

But unfortunately, far too many are not of that character. Or they are partway there and are trying to figure out all of this stuff.

This book is intended for those who are willing to try—to take a hard look at their own internal biases and preconceptions of history and people, and to try and overcome those and see the world and Indigenous cultures and communities not as pan-Indian or homogenous but as unique cultures and people who deserve respect. A world where Indigenous rights should be fully acknowledged, both in law and in practice, and where Indigenous Peoples deserve the support and allyship of the resource sector. As allies, we all have an opportunity to move forward and repair the harm of past attitudes, biases, colonial practices, and laws and to work to realize a sustainable future that benefits all of humanity.

2

Educate Yourself

THIS CHAPTER is meant to provide you with a glimpse of areas in which you can increase your knowledge. You need to learn whose land you are living and working on and what their history is. You need to understand that decolonization, which includes understanding the history of Indigenous Peoples, is everyone's work. Educating yourself is a step forward in that work, and it includes reflecting on your privilege and seeking ways in which you can be supportive and become a true ally.

Education and knowledge about Indigenous cultures, practices, and history could be a multivolume set of books unto itself, and, indeed, there are many that attempt to provide this information. Our effort here is not to try and replicate that but rather to provide some information and references to key issues that are particularly relevant when it comes to the relationship between resource industries and Indigenous communities. We know that in presenting this, there is so much that is left out. However, our main message to our readers is that regardless of where you are in the world, where you are working and the people you are working with, take the time to get to know them, their histories, their concerns, and their hopes for the future. And through this, you will create the possibility of a meaningful relationship.

We are going to begin this discussion with a particularly poignant example of recent history that has caused real harm, as told by Mike. This is a story that involves the largest religion in the world, a federal government complicit in all that took place, and the unmarked graves of thousands of children as young as three years old. It is also a story of how real accountability remains elusive and how that continues to prevent true reconciliation from being realized.

The Vatican, Residential Schools, and the Search for Accountability

MIKE: Over the last seven years, I have been invited to be part of a small group of mining industry executives, multi-faith groups, nongovernmental organizations (NGOs), and civil society representatives who met at the Vatican with senior members of the Catholic Church. This included His Holiness Pope Francis, in what were known as "Days of Reflection." The first of these meetings was in September 2013 and the most recent in May of 2019.

This work was in keeping with Pope Francis's efforts to engage with leaders of industry and civil society on the critical issues of our time, chief among those being climate change, the environment, poverty alleviation, and responsible resource development.

The meetings were convened by the Pontifical Council for Justice and Peace (now known as the Dicastery for Promoting Integral Human Development) and led by His Eminence Cardinal Peter Turkson.

The discussions in these meetings were honest and direct, and stories were told by leaders from communities that had been impacted both positively and negatively by the activities of resource companies. Environmental issues, poverty, corruption, Indigenous rights, human rights, and prior and informed consent were all topics on the table for consideration. The goal of the discussions was to identify strategies to move the resource sector forward toward a more sustainable future. Given that in the room, there were the most senior leaders of some of the largest resource companies in the world, including Anglo American, who initially sponsored this work, BHP, Rio Tinto, De Beers, and Newmont, among others, as well as multi-faith church and NGO leaders who engage significantly on these issues globally, the opportunity for meaningful dialogue was very much there.

I should note that I am not Catholic, although I do consider myself a Christian. In being invited to participate in meetings with the senior leaders of a two-thousand-year-old organization that counts 1.3 billion people as members, I really did not know what to expect. And when we convened our early discussions in the building that housed the Pontifical Academy of Sciences, where the famous astronomer Galileo was a frequent guest, it was certainly intriguing to consider what might be possible in this. I note with some irony that it was reportedly here, in 1616, that Galileo was subjected to an inquisition into heliocentrism and was declared formally heretical for his theories and teachings that the Earth revolved around the sun. This is a good reminder that new ideas can face resistance, and change is often slow when it comes to new ways of thinking within large institutions.

I believe our work in this group over these years was useful and led to some meaningful insights into how the resource sector can continue to improve and work to ensure a more sustainable future.

However, there is another more recent side to this that we struggle with and remain deeply concerned about. And, given the intent of this book and the subject that Christy and I are writing about, it is particularly relevant here.

The history of the relationship between the Catholic Church and Indigenous Peoples can be challenging in many parts of the world. Whether it's Central and South America, Africa, or North America, there are many examples of colonialism and religious efforts that caused real harm to local Indigenous communities. An example of this was brought into sharp view recently in Canada when hundreds of unmarked graves of children who attended Catholic-run residential schools were found on school grounds. Estimates from Indigenous and government assessments have put the number of children who died at these schools—from the late 1800s until the last school closed in 1996—at between four thousand and six thousand.

It is a painful and difficult part of the history of Canada. And for the families and for those who survived being forcibly taken from their homes and subjected to sexual and physical abuse and neglect, what happened is all too recent.

The issue that we would like to raise for this discussion is in regard to the response, or lack of response, of the Church and the Government of Canada to what happened at these schools—and how this example of lack of institutional accountability and harm continues to point to the divide between words, truth, and actual reconciliation with Indigenous Peoples in Canada and globally.

Background

In May 2021, stories first appeared in local and national media outlets about the discovery of some 215 bodies of children as young as three years old on the grounds of the Kamloops Indian Residential School. This school is in the interior of BC, about a four-hour drive from Vancouver, and was operated between 1893 and 1978. It was run by the Missionary Oblates of Mary Immaculate of the Catholic Church, and Indigenous children from the region were sent there, many without the consent of their families.

The graves were discovered using a technology called "ground-penetrating radar." When news broke about the discovery, the story exploded quickly around the world. More stories followed about other schools across the country where Indigenous children were taken and never returned home. Often no explanations were provided to families about what happened, no bodies were returned, and no one was ever held accountable.

Now, we are not sure if it was the combination of the world being in the middle of a pandemic, the fact that it was children, or just the sheer number of graves involved, but this became front-page news not just locally but globally. People who had never thought much about Indigenous issues took an interest in this story, and many questions were being asked. How could this happen? What role did the various institutions play in allowing this? Did this really happen in Canada? Memorials sprung up around the country, with 215 tiny children's shoes placed at the feet of many of them as a symbol of those who died. It was tough stuff and very emotional for many Indigenous and non-Indigenous people.

The reality, though, is that for Indigenous Peoples in Canada, none of this was news. Just a few years earlier, a national commission looking at Indigenous issues in the country had identified the record of the Church and the government on this and estimated the number of children who died at these same schools. The commission, in their final report, spoke of the tragedy and its impact on survivors and their families. They called for investigations of these unmarked graves to be carried out and restitution to be paid to survivors. But there was little attention paid to their calls at the time in mainstream media, and most Canadians had little knowledge of it.

Christy and I both had our own experiences when the Kamloops story came out. Christy spoke with elders and community members who had very personal stories of children who were taken from her own nation and never returned. These were difficult, heartbreaking stories that were still very much in people's everyday language and realities. And I was in this uncomfortable place of working with the Vatican on Indigenous issues, and the resource sector learning about these abuses, and witnessing the weak and ineffective response by the Church to these startling revelations.

A very brief history here, for context.

The Catholic Church was one of three religious groups involved in running the residential school system on behalf of the Government of Canada. The others were the Anglican and United churches. Both of those groups formally apologized (in 1992 and 1981 respectively) for their roles in this and for the harm that was done to Indigenous children.

Individual Catholic bishops have apologized, the Missionary Oblates of Mary Immaculate offered an apology in 1991, and the Canadian Council of Bishops apologized recently in advance of the new Canadian Truth and Reconciliation Day. Pope Benedict XVI met Aboriginal leaders from Canada in 2009 and expressed his "sorrow" for the experiences of the residential school survivors but stopped short of a formal papal apology.

May 2018

Part of my work with the Vatican involved engagement with Indigenous communities in Canada and globally on sustainability issues with the resource sector. Coming back from our meetings in Rome, I reached out to Christy to see about how we might engage in BC and Canada in this work. Both of us spoke with Indigenous leaders and explained what was being proposed, and—surprisingly for me but not for Christy—we did not receive much in the way of a welcoming reception. Christy had warned me about this. The Catholic Church, although still a major part of Indigenous faith in the country, was a polarizing institution for many.

This was long before the Kamloops story.

We continued to try to press this forward over the next two years, but unfortunately momentum seemed to fade. People moved on to other more pressing matters.

Spring 2021

Fast-forward three years almost to the day, and news broke about the discovery of the 215 unmarked graves in Kamloops. This was not a story that was going to go away anytime soon. And it did not, as we have discussed.

I reached out directly to Cardinal Turkson and requested a meeting to discuss the discovery and to try and press upon him that the Church needed to get out in front of this, recognize the seriousness of what had happened here, and set the groundwork for the formal papal apology we had discussed in the near term. The apology would preferably be delivered personally in Canada.

That discussion took place on Thursday, June 2. On Sunday, June 6, in his weekly address on global issues during Mass, Pope Francis acknowledged "with great sorrow" the pain and suffering that had come with the discovery of the mass grave in Kamloops.

I remember feeling proud that I had had some influence on that statement being made and optimistic that this was the start of a true acknowledgement, at the highest level, of the Church taking responsibility for what had taken place in these schools. I believed that could move the focus to true healing and reconciliation. I was encouraged that I could be part of helping to make something happen that was long overdue.

And then it all came crashing down.

The public relations effort from the Church in Canada was, in the early days, lacking on so many levels; it is difficult to describe. An archbishop in eastern Canada denied even knowing about the history of the schools; others publicly stated that the Church was under attack unfairly; and, at the time, other than the statement on June 6, there was nothing formal from the Vatican.

I, along with colleagues of mine, reached out to various senior members of the Church in Canada and did everything we could to encourage them to lead on this matter. Certain members of the Church, like Archbishop J. Michael Miller of Vancouver and Archbishop Donald Bolen of Regina, spoke out publicly and gave sincere recognition to the harm that has been done and the need for significant work to regain trust. Even Archbishop Marcel Damphousse of Ottawa-Cornwall, who originally faced significant criticism in the early days of this based on his lack of knowledge of the issue, changed his position and said publicly that the Pope should offer a formal apology.

So, there was movement, and the seriousness of this was having an effect as public pressure continued to mount.

At the time of this writing, there has been a further step taken: the Vatican issued a statement on October 27, 2021, that the Canadian Conference of Catholic Bishops has invited Pope Francis to travel to Canada in the "context of the long-standing pastoral process of reconciliation with Indigenous peoples." The statement further said the Pope indicated his willingness to do so.

Reflection and Where We Are Now

In our view, the story above is an example of how an institution can discriminate against groups, in this case Indigenous children, and how as a whole, because of conservative views and a fear of real accountability, that same organization can avoid taking full responsibility for the harm that was caused. People in power abused their positions and harmed the most vulnerable, and they have escaped the consequences of their actions.

Further, and most importantly, we would argue that the entire Church failed in this. And that failure caused real harm. This is not just about the actions of a few bad priests or church officials. This is about the institution itself collectively harming the most vulnerable. In an apology from the Conference of Catholic Bishops in September 2021, they refer to the involvement in residential schools of "many Catholic religious communities and dioceses," but without direct reference to the Church overall.

It appears from this as though the bishops continue to believe that while elements of the Church bear responsibility for the schools, the vast majority of Catholics (laity, clergy, and hierarchy) were not involved and hence not responsible. "We did nothing." But we would argue that this is exactly what they *should* be apologizing for. They did nothing while the abuse, neglect, and harm was taking place. As leaders of the institution in Canada, they are responsible.

If, in a corporate context, the board or executive management of a company offered an apology only "for certain elements of their organization that had harmed or killed members of the public" without taking full responsibility for what happened, would that satisfy anyone? They are the leaders and must be responsible for the actions of their entire organization.

Indigenous Peoples and communities the world over have had similar experiences with governments and religious and societal institutions at many points throughout history. And this is one of the reasons why there is so much distrust and anger directed toward those same groups today.

There is no disputing facts or culpability here. Members of the Catholic Church in Canada inflicted real harm on children, and the entire Church bears responsibility. This is not to say that all members of the Church committed this offence, but rather, that they share collective responsibility for the failings of their institution.

And for the Indigenous families who live with the knowledge that their own children, grandchildren, and great-grandchildren died under the care of people and institutions that were supposed to look out for their well-being—and lie in unmarked graves across the country, far from their homes—the immense pain and sadness that must come from that remains.

Deepen Your Understanding

We are going to focus now on several key areas that are critical to deepening your understanding of Indigenous engagement and culture. As with other parts of our work and information being presented, this is not an exhaustive or in-depth review of what it would take to truly educate yourself on these subjects. To do that would take much longer and require a serious commitment on behalf of everyone involved. That is out of reach for most people. So, what is presented and discussed here is intended to provide a strong basis for greater understanding and give you the tools to engage more thoughtfully and with the necessary knowledge to begin building those deeper, more resilient relationships.

Royal Proclamation of 1763

For the Indigenous Peoples of North America, the Royal Proclamation of 1763 issued by King George III is foundational in terms of establishing their relationship with the Crown and ownership of their lands and interests. Following Great Britain's victory over the French and their allies in the Seven Years War, the Royal Proclamation served to issue ownership of North America to King George. In this though, the Royal Proclamation explicitly states that Aboriginal title has existed and continues to exist, and that all land would be considered Aboriginal land unless ceded by treaty. The Proclamation forbade settlers from acquiring or claiming land from Aboriginal occupants unless it had been acquired first by the Crown and then sold to the settlers. The Proclamation further set out that only the Crown could acquire land from Aboriginal peoples.

As noted in a review of the Royal Proclamation by the First Nations Study Program of the University of British Columbia, "most legal and Indigenous scholars recognize the Royal Proclamation as an important first step toward the recognition of existing Aboriginal rights and title, including the right to self-determination." [6]

We would expect that, for most readers, it is relatively easy to see the most glaring issue in this Proclamation by a foreign power in terms of the formerly autonomous Indigenous people of North America. On one hand, the Crown recognizes Aboriginal interests and title and serves to protect those from settlers who no doubt saw this as a land of unlimited opportunity, which is a good thing. But on the other, in this Proclamation, Great Britain and the Crown have established themselves as the masters and final decision-maker in this relationship without any engagement or input from Aboriginal leaders. Much of our current and recent history with respect to Aboriginal land rights, title discussions, and treaties has been materially influenced by this document, which is over 250 years old.

Take Decolonization and Cultural Sensitivity Training

Decolonization requires recognizing your place, power, and inherent privilege in the current colonial framework. This can be difficult, because it can come with tough feelings, including embarrassment, complicity, guilt, shame, helplessness, avoidance, and grief. There are many training opportunities and courses developed by Indigenous experts in this area. Reconciliation and decolonization are complex processes, but they have tangible and doable elements that help them progress. These include:

Intercultural Understanding

Intercultural understanding happens when you can openly, without judgement, observe or learn about another culture distinct from your own. It involves examining the power dynamics that are at work and the ways they have altered knowledge transmission and relationships. Intercultural understanding involves looking at your own positionality and place in those power dynamics.

Territorial Acknowledgements

Some people are confused by declarations at the beginning of events that go something like this: "We would like to acknowledge that we are on the traditional unceded territory of xxx nation." It is good practice to do your research and know whose traditional territory you are on when you are home or at work and when you travel. "Traditional," when used in an acknowledgement or welcome, communicates that the land has been used and occupied by a particular group before col-onization—often for many thousands of years. And "unceded" explains that the land was never formally transferred to the Crown by treaty or any other agreement.

It is also important to understand your intention behind acknowledging traditional territory. Are you just doing it because everyone else does it? Or do you truly understand with sincerity that you are doing business in the traditional territory of a nation or multiple nations? What does that truly mean to you?

Anyone can speak the acknowledgement, but a formal wel-come and/or prayer at an event or gathering must be done by a leader, elder, or member of the particular First Nation on whose land the event is occurring. If you are unsure who that might be, it is okay to ask and seek clarification. The words contained in these acknowledgements and welcomes have meaning and communicate value. As such, it is respectful to stand during a formal welcome and prayer.

Educate Yourself on the History of Indigenous Peoples

Everyone will benefit from investing in education on the diverse and storied history of Indigenous Peoples in the area, region, or country in which you live and work. What you may think are truths or facts could be assumptions or could be affected by the oppressive colonial processes and world sys-tems within which we currently live.

Navigating complex colonial countries like Canada with an attitude and actions of reconciliation means being mindful in what you say and do.

Colonial legislation from the 1800s still legally defines Indigenous Peoples in Canada and other settled coun-tries today. In Canada, the Indian Act affects and controls

Indigenous Peoples in every part of this vast country. It dictates who is considered a legal, status "Indian" and therefore who has access to federal supports and services.

Historically, the Indian Act has prevented First Nations from leaving their reserves, dictated who had the right to vote, indicated that one could lose the ability to vote by becoming a lawyer or doctor, decided when and if cultural ceremonies could be practiced, changed "Indian" names, controlled the band election system, and allowed the government to displace Indigenous communities or expropriate reserve lands as needed.

Most recently, the Act has been amended to remove gender-based discrimination whereby women lost status and rights when they married a non-Indigenous person; their children lost status through gendered classifications, and "status" could not be passed down past a certain generation. Recent amendments have sought to align the Indian Act with the Constitution of Canada and basic human rights. Contrast this with the past, where having even a drop of Indigenous blood prevented people from having full access to Canadian culture and society.

The discussion here is a primarily Canadian example of race-based legislation impacting Indigenous Peoples. The experience in Canada is, however, just one of many around the world. Whether considering the experience of Native Americans, the Aboriginal people of Australia or New Zealand, or the many Indigenous communities of Central and South America. All of these communities have their own histories of colonization and subjugation from the laws of foreign powers. And the impact of those past and current policies, laws, and practices are present in much of the debates over resource development, land ownership, and decision-making today.

Educate Yourself on How Indigenous Peoples Have Transformed the World We Live In

People throughout the world enjoy the fruits of Indigenous contributions without being aware of their origin. The more you research, the more you will realize how much the world has adopted and incorporated Indigenous culture and ingenuity. Many people don't want to pay elders honorariums or monies for knowledge, and yet Indigenous Peoples have changed the world with their knowledge. Indigenous communities feel that their knowledge has been taken from them with no recompense or acknowledgement. As a result, you shouldn't be shocked when communities may not want to share their traditional knowledge.

Some of their contributions are listed here:

CLOTHING: For thousands of years before the arrival of the Europeans, Indigenous Peoples had been developing some of the finest textiles in the world. Today, much of the cotton clothing we wear comes from the cotton that Indigenous Peoples originally produced. Europeans also adopted the clothing dyes that Indigenous Peoples had perfected over thousands of years.

FOOD: Starting thousands of years before Europeans came to the Americas, Indigenous Peoples were experimenting and perfecting agriculture. Europeans depended primarily on grain crops of wheat, rye, barley, and oats. Aside from the occasional side dish of parsnips, turnips, or carrots, Europeans did not have root crops. Grain crops are easy prey for wind, hail, heavy rain, snow, birds, insects, and animals, making them precarious to produce.

Foods that Indigenous Peoples introduced include potatoes, corn, tomatoes, zucchini, artichokes, avocados, squash, and pumpkins; green, yellow, and red peppers; all beans; wild rice; sunflower seeds; peanuts and pecans; papayas; cranberries; chocolate and vanilla; mints; curry and paprika; chilies; maple syrup, chewing gum, and more.

POLITICS: The Iroquois Confederacy is the oldest participatory democracy in the world, and elements of it were included in the US Constitution. For example, members could not hold more than one position, there were processes to remove leaders from the Confederacy, they had two branches dedicated to different law passing, they had rules about who could declare war, and they managed a balance of power between the entire Confederacy and the member tribes.

MEDICINE: From the very first contact, Europeans recognized that the Indigenous Peoples held the key to the world's most sophisticated pharmacy. Indigenous Peoples taught Europeans to use arnica to sooth muscles, to chew on willow bark as a pain reliever, to use cedar to prevent scurvy, and to apply dandelion sap to remove warts. All of these remedies were exploited and are used today by pharmaceutical companies.

Use Correct and Unharmful Terminology

The history between Indigenous Peoples and what is now Canada is complex, and it has been paternalistic and damaging. As a result, the terminology that is used can be powerful. Indigenous Peoples have been called Indian, First Nations, Aboriginal, and Indigenous; these terms can carry colonial histories, embedded power dynamics, racism, and misrepresentations.

Indigenous communities are increasingly using their languages and their Indigenous names to identify themselves. In this case, terminology has the power of self-identification, a reconnection to the past, and a disassociation from colonial power structures.

The terms "Aboriginal" and "Indigenous" are usually not offensive; however, the most respectful approach is to be as specific as possible when using a term. Referring to a community by their self-identified or preferred name is a sign of respect. Fear of using the "wrong" term should never stifle important dialogue. If you are unsure, asking for clarification is respected.

CHRISTY: Although all of these terms are contentious, as they have been applied by colonizers, my personal preference is to say that I am an Indigenous woman from the K'ómoks First Nation. The umbrella term "Indigenous" is the term used in the United Nations Declaration on the Rights of Indigenous Peoples, and it can also be used in a global context. It generally refers to people of long settlement and connection to specific lands, and in the Canadian context it includes all Aboriginal groups.

Educate Yourself on How to Develop a Harm-Free, Trauma-Informed Approach to Dialogue and Your Actions

What Is Harm?

When we talk about the creation of harm in this chapter, we are referring to taking what could be a safe space for dialogue and transforming it (sometimes unintentionally) into a harmful space. This includes bringing ego to the table, making participants feel too intimidated to ask questions or raise issues, devaluing others' experiences by framing the company or yourself as a victim, and reacting with white fragility. Many people will shut down and not engage if they feel as though a place, a conversation, or a meeting is not safe and free from harm.

Bullies, misogynists, and people with uniformed, racist points of view—they exist in society and in business. And yes, in the resource sector. Their actions and words can cause harm to Indigenous and non-Indigenous people, and for those in a leadership position, it is critical to recognize those people and attitudes in advance. Action needs to be taken (and be seen as being taken) so that those who may have experienced the harm can feel safe to engage.

We know that some of you might not see yourselves or the people you are working with as being part of this type of discussion. But have you said or heard something like the following? "Yes, Bob is a bit rough around the edges. But he is a good guy and does not mean any harm."

"Rough around the edges" is okay as long as Bob is treating people with respect and building a culture of safety and openness to differing opinions. That is what constitutes a harm-free workplace.

What Is Trauma-Informed?

A trauma-informed approach to dialogue and your subsequent actions are extremely important when working with Indigenous communities. This approach supports healing and intends to do no further harm or re-traumatization. This includes being aware of potential ways that your biases, values, language, and actions can cause harm, and ways that trauma can manifest in reactions and relationships.

CHRISTY: A personal example of this occurred when I was working for a company that was building a mining camp in a remote northern region of northern BC. The company discovered that the camp triggered trauma for residential school survivors. As a result, employees hired from the nations worked a shift and never returned. Retention would have been better had a trauma-informed approach to engagement and development been implemented, including sharing plans well in advance.

Language

More than seventy Aboriginal languages were reported in the 2016 Census of Canada.[7] Language shapes the way that people think about and interact with the world. For many people, their ancestral language is integral to their cultural expression and continuity. Aboriginal languages in Canada have been evolving in this land over generations, and they reflect rich and diverse histories, landscapes, cultures, and knowledge. Many Aboriginal languages are unique to Canada and aren't spoken anywhere else in the world.

Past events have significantly harmed the vitality of Aboriginal languages in Canada. These include the residential school system, under which generations of Aboriginal children were not permitted to speak their Aboriginal mother tongues.[8]

It is often said that learning another culture's language is a great show of respect. So why is this not done more often when resource companies are engaging with Indigenous communities? And given the histories we have discussed here regarding colonization, consider how you would feel as an Indigenous person if, despite the importance of language to you, the people who wished to build a relationship with you did not take the time to even learn the basics?

Consider if you were going to do a project in South or Central America. Would you not either learn Spanish or Portuguese or, at a minimum, have people on your team with that ability?

There are many resources available to access Indigenous languages today that were not formerly available. Take the time to find them and learn at least some. It will not be easy, because they are not spoken in mainstream culture and may sound strange to your ears. But your efforts will show that you do care, are taking the time to try and understand, and are trying not to cause harm. That is worth it, and you will be richer for your efforts.

Summary

As we noted at the outset, educating yourself is critical to understanding and appreciating the people and their land upon which you are wanting to work. To be successful in building meaningful, resilient relationships with Indigenous Peoples, you need to understand where they are coming from— what their history is and the struggles and successes they have had. And, in so doing, you will have an opportunity to create a deeper connection that can withstand the ups and downs of time and adversity.

So, spend the time to better understand the people you are working with—who they are and what they have gone through. What they hope for and what they fear. What they love and what makes them smile. What they like and what they detest. Most of all, show them respect and assure them that you have made an effort to understand who they are. You will still make mistakes for sure. You may say the wrong thing or act in a way that is unintended and could upset someone. But if you have taken the time to truly appreciate and understand someone and you are coming from a good place, then the chances are you will be forgiven.

3

Consultation
Is a Legal
Requirement

FOR THOSE working in the resource sector, understanding what is required for true consultation with Indigenous communities has been difficult. It has evolved over time, as practices and legal definitions have changed in line with direction from the courts, international conventions, and the recognition of the important role Indigenous communities play in decision-making regarding land use, environmental protection, and resource exploitation.

For those who work in industry, it has also been difficult to understand what responsibility *they* have versus the Crown or government who, at least in Canada, have the statutory and legal obligation to consult. This is particularly true when those same government agencies, with their clearly defined obligation for consultation, defer to industry to fulfill consultation requirements because of staffing or resource limitations.

For First Nations and Indigenous communities in Canada and elsewhere in the world, in principle, consultation means that they are directly engaged and consulted with on decisions that affect their lands, resources, people, or future—and that that engagement is serious, fulsome, timely, honest, and legitimate.

It is not a "box-checking exercise" but rather something much more involved that ensures these communities are engaged in decisions, permits, or approvals before they are made. And it is the material responsibility of industry to demonstrate that this has happened.

In the following chapter, we will outline some of the key aspects of consultation and decision-making that constitute the obligation for free, prior, and informed consent, also known as FPIC. We will also look at the evolution of the permitting and environmental assessment process in Canada and how Indigenous engagement, in many places around the world, has become the cornerstone of how this now works.

As with other large and complicated subjects discussed in this book, it is not possible to go in depth into what can often be complex legal and policy-related areas. So what we have done is try to frame the main points that are critical to understanding the issue and then provide references to resources that you can access to find out more.

What Is the Duty to Consult?

In Canada, the duty and obligation to consult have been defined legally through several landmark decisions from the Supreme Court, including Haida, Taku River, Mikisew Cree, Little Salmon Carmacks, and Rio Tinto.

As outlined in the Supreme Court of Canada Rio Tinto case, "the duty to consult arises when the Crown has knowledge, real or constructive, of the potential existence of the

Aboriginal right or title and contemplates conduct that might adversely affect it." As well, "the duty to consult is a constitutional duty invoking the honour of the Crown. It must be met."

And further, as defined by the Province of BC, "the Province is legally obligated to consult and accommodate First Nations, where required, on land and resource decisions that could impact their Indigenous interests. While the Province is responsible for ensuring adequate and appropriate consultation and accommodation, it may involve the proponent in the procedural aspects of consultation."

So, consultation with Indigenous Peoples is the obligation of the Crown, as represented by the government. They must discuss all matters and decisions that have the potential to adversely impact on Aboriginal rights or title, whether they knowingly exist or have the potential to exist. From the perspective of any activity associated with the resource industry, pretty much every decision that the government will make must meet this test and will require consultation.

So that is our starting point. But what does that mean for industry? At the most basic level, it means that the government is required by law to engage on all material decisions that they are making. So every permit, every licence, every authorization that they are granting to a proponent must be cleared by the Indigenous community that has an interest in the project area prior to a decision being made.

Some in industry have defaulted to the idea that this is indeed a government-to-government responsibility, and so they are just bystanders to this legal obligation and process, which is a mistake—not a legal mistake but a practical one.

The fact is the government does not have the resources to engage and consult at the level required for every project and every decision. It is just not possible—particularly given the complexity of extractive projects, which can involve hundreds of different permits, assessments, and licences. This means that industry must step up and actively participate in the process of consultation and engagement. Every conversation must be recorded. Logs must be kept, issues must be raised, and whether or not they were resolved must be detailed in a formal record. That information needs to be well organized, accurate, and available for review by both Indigenous representatives and government. It forms part of the official record and will support government decision-making.

This does not absolve government of its ultimate responsibility, but it does support the overall dialogue and discussion on decision-making.

Free, Prior, and Informed Consent and the United Nations Declaration on the Rights of Indigenous Peoples

Free, prior, and informed consent (FPIC) is a right of Indigenous Peoples, and it is recognized under international law; it derives from the right of self-determination; the right to freely pursue economic, social, and cultural development; and individual human rights. Its status as a right has been affirmed by various human rights bodies and relevant jurisprudence.

This right has gained recognition globally and has been adopted as a core principle of some elements of the resource sector, including the global mining and minerals industry. In a recent position statement on Indigenous Peoples and mining, the International Council on Mining and Metals (ICMM) outlined:

> In ICMM's view, FPIC comprises a process, and an outcome. Through this process Indigenous Peoples are: (i) able

to freely make decisions without coercion, intimidation or manipulation; (ii) given sufficient time to be involved in project decision making before key decisions are made and impacts occur; and (iii) fully informed about the project and its potential impacts and benefits.

The outcome is that Indigenous Peoples can give or withhold their consent to a project, through a process that strives to be consistent with their traditional decision-making processes while respecting internationally recognised human rights and is based on good faith negotiation.[9]

The United Nations Declaration on the Rights of Indigenous Peoples (UNDRIP) was adopted by the UN's General Assembly in 2007. UNDRIP explicitly mentions the right of FPIC in the following circumstances:

- Before relocation (Article 10).

- Prior to the use of Indigenous Peoples' cultural, intellectual, religious, and spiritual property (Article 11).

- Prior to implementation of legislative or administrative measures that could affect Indigenous Peoples (Article 19).

- Prior to use of lands (Article 28).

- Prior to storage or disposal of hazardous materials on Indigenous Peoples' lands (Article 29).

- Prior to state approval of "any project affecting their lands or territories and other resources, particularly in connection with the development, utilization or exploitation of mineral, water or other resources" (Article 32).

UNDRIP was adopted into legislation by the Province of BC in 2020, and on June 16, 2021, Canada's Senate voted to pass Bill C-15, the United Nations Declaration on the Rights of Indigenous Peoples Act (the UNDRIP Act or the Act), into law.

With respect to the resource sector, there is very little the industry does that will not in some way affect the rights and interests of one or more Indigenous communities. Access, the project itself, the transportation of materials, and the regional environmental impacts—all of these have the potential to impact on at least one or possibly multiple Indigenous communities. And, under these new policy and legal obligations associated with FPIC and UNDRIP, how industry and government take these rights and interests into account is a significant part of any development.

We cannot emphasize enough how big of a deal this shift in policy, legislation, and obligations is with respect to industry and government when it comes to how much FPIC matters in practice. Whether it is a new natural gas well site being developed, a mineral exploration project under consideration that requires a drilling permit, or a new piece of infrastructure needed to support a project, every aspect of industrial development that affects Indigenous interests will require that consent. For readers interested in learning more about this, an excellent resource is "The Practice of FPIC" published by RESOLVE, which can be found at fpicdialogue.org.

Environmental Assessments, Permitting, and Indigenous Engagement

It is hard to overstate the rising influence and importance of Indigenous engagement in the assessment and permitting of resource industry projects. To say it is the determining factor between success and failure would not be an understatement in Canada, many parts of the United States, and, increasingly, in developing nations. Only a limited number of countries' national Environmental Impact Assessment (EIA) legislation includes specific provisions related to the participation of Indigenous Peoples. However, we would offer that it is just a matter of time, and this will evolve and change in the years ahead.

UNDRIP and free, prior, and informed consent is part of that, as is the role and policies of international lending institutions like the International Finance Corporation (IFC) and key policy guidance like the Equator Principles (EPs) and Environmental, Social, and Corporate Governance (ESG).

For the purposes of this discussion, a couple of examples can be helpful in terms of framing what the current state of practice is, and they may point to what will happen globally as FPIC, in particular, becomes the norm.

Seeking Consensus: The New British Columbia Environmental Assessment Act

In November 2018, the Government of BC introduced a new Environmental Assessment Act, which provides a mechanism by which to review major projects and assess their impacts and affects. This new EA Act differs in several material ways from earlier legislation, particularly regarding early and ongoing Indigenous engagement.

Early engagement is the front end of the process—the time at which government, Indigenous representatives, and the public are made aware of a proposed development and asked formally to identify any concerns they might have. To begin the process, the proponent prepares what is known as an Initial Project Description (IPD) report that these groups use to inform their opinion on what is being considered.

The IPD is fairly broad in scope but has a sufficient level of detail that people can assess the concept and understand what the impacts and opportunities are likely to be. Think of it as a summary report that tells you what the project is, where it is, who is involved, and what the impacts are likely to be. It also provides enough information to generate informed opinions as to whether this is a good idea or not—or at least enough to know what might be being considered and whether it is important to be involved going forward.

The key in this is that to be able to proceed to the next phases of the environmental assessment (EA) process, there is a requirement to reach consensus with all the major stakeholders, of which Indigenous communities are a major part. Failure to achieve that will mean that the project proponent will need to go back to the beginning in considering their concepts for a development or possibly reconsider the entire undertaking if a clear path is not visible in terms of being able to move forward.

From a government perspective, this seems smart, as it provides an early opportunity to evaluate whether a project is going to face serious resistance or concerns. Rather than proceeding forward for (oftentimes) years and then having to manage a fractious and antagonistic process, this provides an opportunity to evaluate what the real concerns are and work to either address those or make the decision that it is not in the public interest to proceed.

Power Shift

Consider the power shift that has taken place here, as it is quite profound, and it has not received the level of attention it probably should have. Indeed, this is not just an isolated policy change for BC but rather globally, as local communities, be they Indigenous or not, have a greater say in what takes place in and around their communities.

In the not too distant past, a proponent would approach a major extractive type of project—a mine, a gas development, or a new transportation or power corridor—with a view that there was an assessment and permitting process to follow, and yes, it would take time, but the outcome, if they did a good job, was rarely in doubt. Of course, there are a few exceptions, but for the most part the outcome was ultimately reasonably predictable.

What has changed here, though, is that now there is a referendum taking place right at the beginning as to whether the community—and in Canada in particular, the Indigenous communities of the area—is interested in a project at all. And there is a real chance that the answer is no in certain cases, which means consensus cannot be reached. Which then means it will be difficult politically and practically for a government to proceed. Some in industry may believe their projects are important enough that the government will assert its will and power to push a project through, despite local objections. In our view, which is backed up by a number of recent decisions by governments in North America, thinking that is likely wishful thinking and will not be realized, except in the rarest of cases.

Beyond this stage, the environmental assessment and permitting process has numerous steps and points at which Indigenous engagement will happen. Some of this will be "government to government," and some of this will be the responsibility of the proponent.

What is clear from all of this is that the views of Indigenous communities on any proposed development project at a certain scale will be critical.

Indigenous-Led Environmental Assessments

In recognition of the limitations of and complaints from Indigenous communities and leaders about how governments have, or have not, exercised their duty to consult, and consistent with the movement of Indigenous Peoples to have a much greater say over activities within the territories, in recent years there has been a movement toward Indigenous communities leading the impact assessment process themselves. This is not just as another party in a government-led process; it is designing a process that aims to reconcile Indigenous and national or provincial/state laws.

Two recent examples of this approach come from BC, where the Squamish Nation and the Tsleil-Waututh Nation have developed processes for the evaluation of projects within their traditional territories. The Squamish Nation has developed the Squamish Nation Process to assert their rights and title and to protect their traditional lands and waters. And similarly, the Tsleil-Waututh Nation has created a process whereby assessments are carried out under their stewardship policy in order to provide the nation with the information needed to make informed decisions on whether to consent to a proposal or withhold support.

In the case of the Squamish Nation, this process was used in their evaluation of a proposed LNG export terminal within their territory. Their assessment concluded with the company, Woodfibre LNG, being advised that they would require agreement to thirteen specific conditions imposed on them by the nation in order to proceed. The company subsequently agreed to those conditions, and at this time, the project is poised to proceed.

The Tsleil-Waututh Nation issued their own independent assessment of the Trans Mountain Pipeline and Tanker Expansion Proposal (TMX). This assessment was guided by their stewardship policy and in this case concluded that the TMX proposal does not represent the best use of Tsleil-Waututh territory and its water, land, air, and resources to satisfy the needs of their ancestors and future generations.

Not all Indigenous communities will have the capacity or resources to undertake assessments such as this. They are expensive, time-consuming, and demand a significant commitment of community resources. So, in the short to medium term, it is likely that except in the case of major projects, full Indigenous-led assessments will be rare.

However, this is the direction in which things are moving, and we expect to see many more examples like this in the years ahead.

Documentation Is Key

Some advice we would offer to proponents is to make sure you have a robust system in place to document all of your engagement and consultation. This includes every meeting, every material discussion, how you have resolved issues, and the dialogue you have had with the chief and council.

You may run across some nations who state that they want it on the record that this is not to be considered "consultation"—that they will still document the conversations and ensure that everyone follows through on action items, but in honour of the nation, they do not wish to submit those as part of the consultation record to the government.

This information will be important in validating with the government that your consultation obligations have been met. It will also likely be used by the government to demonstrate that their obligations have been met as well before they make decisions that may impact an Indigenous community.

Sometimes the Answer Will Be No

Legal obligations to consult. UNDRIP. Free, prior, and informed consent. These all lead to real change from the way things have been done in the past when looking at resource development and major projects.

Indigenous interests are no longer represented in the list of stakeholders whose concerns need to be "taken into account." It is now a much higher bar and level of consideration being applied in law, both in public policy and in practice. Simply, if Indigenous communities with a legitimate interest in a project area are not on board with what is proposed, it is highly unlikely that a project will proceed. This is the power shift we have been talking about, and it is real.

Is that considered a veto? In a legal sense, no. Government can still make decisions that are considered in the broader "public or national interest" but that might be contrary to the wishes of Indigenous Peoples. And in other less developed or progressive countries in the world, this continues to happen on a regular basis.

However, in a practical sense, we would argue that it has become essentially a veto. This is because the time, political capital, effort, adverse public sentiment, possible legal challenges, and impact to the reputation of the company that will result if government and industry proceed on a development without the consent of Indigenous communities can make the economics and legitimacy of a project untenable.

Legally, though, governments have been quick to say that FPIC does not confer a veto of economic development—that the Crown or the state or federal government has the right to make decisions about land and resource development, particularly on the grounds of "national interest." This is what happened in Canada recently with the TMX pipeline, which some Indigenous groups opposed, but the Government of Canada decided to move forward with the project despite this. And those projects will happen sometimes. We would argue, though, that they will become increasingly rare, as the political risk is just too high and so few projects reach the level of national importance.

The fact is, if an Indigenous community is expressly against a project for legitimate reasons of infringement on the rights and/or interests of their community, both now and in the future, or for material environmental concerns, then it is highly unlikely a project will go ahead. There are few governments that will seek to oppose that based purely on legal grounds of jurisdiction. And with UNDRIP now law in Canada, those legal grounds in many cases no longer exist, at least in this country, which is a real shift in the dynamic of industry, government, and capital allocation globally. The reality of this has only started to settle in over the past few years, and we would expect some high-profile altercations for those that have not fully appreciated the shift that has taken place.

Summary

Government and industry have a legal obligation to consult with Indigenous communities regarding decisions that impact on their rights and interests. The United Nations Declaration of the Rights of Indigenous Peoples (UNDRIP) is now law in Canada and is increasingly being referred to globally in defining the rights of Indigenous Peoples.

Indigenous engagement is critical within modern permitting processes and can be a major determining factor in whether a project is approved or rejected. Sometimes the answer will be no, and this is something that industry has rarely had to face over history, except in more extreme circumstances. This represents a material shift in power and influence over decision-making, and it demands a much higher level of engagement and involvement with Indigenous communities in resource project planning and development.

4

Land, Water,
and Seven
Generations

THIS CHAPTER is about the environment—about the land,
the water, and the plants and creatures that inhabit those
places. It is also about time. In looking at these elements,
the intent is to provide some insight into how an Indigenous
perspective on them changes the context of what extractive
companies, western science, and typical permitting and assessment processes will typically apply.

As with all of our writing here, this is our interpretation of
these important issues only, and we fully recognize that there
may be other interpretations, beliefs, and views.

Indigenous Perspective of the Environment

A gentle reminder of what you learned in Chapter 1: assuming pan-Indianism will get you thrown out of a meeting. This
includes a pan-Indianism belief that we all think the same

when it comes to time, the environment, and how we steward the land.

There are a lot of references on how Indigenous Peoples and communities view nature, the environment, Turtle Island, and Mother Earth. One reference that captures this well comes from Canada's Assembly of First Nations in reference to honouring water:

> Water is the most life sustaining gift on Mother Earth and is the interconnection among all living beings. Water sustains us, flows between us, within us, and replenishes us. Water is the blood of Mother Earth and, as such, cleanses not only herself, but all living things. Water comes in many forms and all are needed for the health of Mother Earth and for our health. The sacred water element teaches us that we can have great strength to transform even the tallest mountain while being soft, pliable, and flexible. Water gives us the spiritual teaching that we too flow into the Great Ocean at the end of our life journey. Water shapes the land and gives us the great gifts of the rivers, lakes, ice, and oceans. Water is the home of many living things that contribute to the health and well-being of everything not in the water.[10]

Reading this perhaps makes it easier to understand why the activities of the extractive industry can be a challenge for Indigenous communities. Altering landscapes, diverting waterways, effluent going into rivers or streams—all of these activities will, by their very nature, affect Indigenous Peoples and the territories they steward.

It almost seems as if the two views of the world and the environment could be irreconcilable. And in some cases, they are. Understanding these different perspectives is at the heart of the challenge that must be faced when considering the practice of resource extraction and use.

What is critical for industry and for those who are non-Indigenous is to gain a better understanding of how Indigenous Peoples see the activities associated with extracting natural resources and the resultant impacts to the environment. Every nation will have differing views; some will employ technical support so tables can communicate in the same technical language, even though many elders hold the same knowledge via teachings and cellular memory. Indigenous communities all have varying concepts of time and decision-making processes. This, too, must be understood.

Impacts on Mother Earth, Turtle Island, are very personal and felt deeply by many—not something easily explained away by detection limits, environmental impact assessments, or water quality models. Different approaches that consider values and different scales of time are often needed. Considering how the health of ecosystems might be affected by an extractive project not just in terms of mg/L of metals in water, for example, but also working to provide assurances that the life-sustaining element in which that ecosystem functions will not be harmed.

Traditional Ecological Knowledge

Traditional Ecological Knowledge (TEK) represents experience acquired over thousands of years of direct human contact with the environment. The term TEK came into widespread use in the 1980s.[11] Another term that is commonly used for this is "Indigenous Knowledge" or IK.

There is a significant body of writing and discussion of what TEK is, how that information is gathered, and how this knowledge can be used to influence and support good decision-making around resource extraction projects. Indeed, the use of TEK or Indigenous Knowledge is a core concept within the new Canadian Impact Assessment Act, the Canadian Energy Regulator Act, and various other pieces of provincial and federal legislation.[12]

For the purpose of this discussion, consider TEK and IK as the culmination of multiple generations of learning, experience, and knowledge gained by Indigenous Peoples about the lands, waters, ecology, wildlife, fish, and climate in which they have lived. Traditional knowledge is usually shared among elders, healers, hunters, and gatherers, and it is passed on to the next generation through ceremonies, territories, or teachings.[13] For those in the resource sector, this knowledge and those who keep it should be fully acknowledged and respected. This includes the stories, the facts, and the history of their people, which also shape their world view.

There is still a lot of work to do in understanding how best to incorporate this knowledge into the design, assessment, and permitting of resource projects. That journey will likely be a long one and will be unique from one project and one community to the next.

What is critical, though, is that TEK and IK are acknowledged as being both important and legitimate; the source of that knowledge deserves full respect and recognition as having a role and an influence over how projects and their possible impacts are considered; and TEK and IK should be recorded and preserved in a confidential manner for the benefit of the people it is gathered from and their future generations.

Generational Planning

Indigenous communities and people think in much longer time frames than non-Indigenous people do. Indigenous decision-making considers our children, our grandchildren, and their children. A resource company's use of the land is short, and after a project is finished, these communities remain.

Indigenous communities are the stewards of the land and always have been. Not for just now but for generations and beyond. Many nations plan for seven generations into the future. The Seventh Generation Principle takes its name from the Great Law of the Haudenosaunee, the founding document of the Iroquois confederacy, the oldest living participatory democracy on Earth. It is based on an ancient Iroquois philosophy that: "In our every deliberation, we must consider the impact of our decisions on the next seven generations."[14]

So what does this concept mean in the context of the resource industry and western-style decision-making? Well, it means we have a real challenge when it comes to reconciling a two-hundred-plus-year perspective with the normally relatively short-term views of industry and government. And that can lead to challenges when it comes to understanding one another's perspective.

For example, most project proponents are looking for Indigenous communities to make decisions relatively quickly. This can be counterintuitive and problematic if what is needed is to consider the impact of that decision on seven future generations. That type of consideration takes time, study, and discussion. We live in a "hurry up" world of expediency, which can be directly at odds with traditional decision-making practices.

That is not always the case if an Indigenous community has a clear view and a plan around how they envision economic development within their traditional territory. Some projects will fit with that future, while others may not. But for the many communities that have not yet done that work or reached a consensus on what the future of their community should look like, major new projects that will be part of shaping that future (for both the good and bad) can be problematic. This work may require a material evaluation of how that future might look and whether they should put their support behind what is envisioned.

Taking that into consideration and embracing responsibility takes time. Many of us have trouble seeing beyond a few weeks or years, and businesses often work on quarterly returns rather than reflecting on what their company may or may not be seven generations into the future. Most, if not all, will be long gone by then.

This process takes work, and it forces us to broaden our horizons and our understanding of what the future may look like, the impact a particular project may or may not have, and the legacy that may be left behind.

An Opportunity

Rather than looking at this as negative, considering decisions and projects in this longer time frame may also be a valuable opportunity for project proponents and Indigenous communities to build authentic relationships. Using this perspective from the beginning of planning and engineering a project provides a chance to consider the legacy of a development and how it can be leveraged for future benefits far beyond the typical ten or twenty years that are normally considered.

For certain extractive projects, looking at these decisions and outcomes on a much longer time scale could be quite positive. Consider the rehabilitative power of nature and its ability to recover from human-made and natural impacts. That alone may allow well-designed projects to gain support from Indigenous communities, if it can be shown that short-term effects can be countered by the social and economic benefits of the development and that there is the ability to return lands and waters to productive and healthy capacity in the medium to longer term.

There is much to explore within Indigenous perspectives of time and decision-making when it comes to resource projects, how they are designed and developed, and lasting positive impacts that will benefit seven generations.

Let's finish this chapter with a story from Mike to help with this discussion.

Aquarius Project Public Meeting— Timmins, Ontario, Spring 1996

There were maybe forty or so people in attendance at a local community hall and ice rink known as the McIntyre Arena in a historic part of Timmins known as Schumacher. A small community of a few dozen houses, Schumacher sits in the shadow of the headframe of the famous McIntyre gold mine. One of Canada's most iconic and largest mines, the McIntyre produced eleven million ounces of gold over seventy-eight years and employed thousands of people. The McIntyre Arena also produced the famed Toronto Maple Leafs forward and six-time Stanley Cup winner Frank "Big M" Mahovlich, who went on to become a Canadian senator.

People were there to learn about a mining company known as Echo Bay Mines and the plans the company had for a nearby project known as Aquarius. A proposed open-pit gold mine that happened to be located on the edge (like, literally on the edge) of a relatively large local water body known as Night Hawk Lake, Aquarius was to be another mining operation in this historic gold mining region of northern Canada.

Echo Bay had spent many millions of dollars exploring, designing, and testing a "freeze wall" that was proposed to surround the open pit. The wall was necessary because there were a hundred metres of saturated glacial alluvium over-laying Precambrian bedrock, where groundwater could flow through it into the area of the gold deposit that was to be excavated. Without the freeze wall, water would flow uncontrolled from Night Hawk Lake into the open pit as it was developed and operated.

Now, it is fairly easy to imagine the potential problems should the wall not function as planned or fail for some reason. The lake itself is quite large and deep and could fill the entire planned open pit easily, representing both a serious safety and an environmental risk. The lake was also used regularly by First Nations and locals for fishing and recreation throughout the year.

The project had been advancing through a comprehensive permitting process for some time, and the company was doing its best to try and address any concerns that the public and regulators might have.

Fast-forward to 2021, twenty-five years later, and the Aquarius deposit remains undeveloped. This during a time when gold prices have gone up ten-fold and there has been significant development of new gold mines in the area. So, you know how that part of the story ends.

This story is not about the permitting and development of the Aquarius project per se, however. What it is about is the beginning of some serious questioning of unbridled industrial development by Indigenous Peoples in Canada, where that comes from, and how racist stereotypes influence perspectives.

Let's go back to the public meeting we started with.

Most of the audience sat toward the back or stood around the edges of the room. The rows of chairs near the front were left empty, as if this was the last performance of an unpopular school play. Early on I noticed that near the front of the audience was one older gentleman who I thought may be of

First Nations descent. He was dressed in jeans, a heavy coat, and a baseball cap. He appeared to be there on his own. There was nothing unique about this to me, as I had spent the previous years working in the Arctic and in BC, where Indigenous involvement in resource development projects was common and expected.

As the meeting advanced, the company representatives and their consultants worked through a presentation on the proposed Aquarius project. The engineering experts assured the audience of the soundness of their planning and engineering, and their environmental consultants outlined the extensive studies they had done over the previous several years on Night Hawk Lake and the surrounding environs. There was a detailed discussion on the freeze wall, how it would work, and the safeguards in place to protect the lake and the area's groundwater resources. The presentation finished with a discussion about the amount of money the company intended to spend in the coming years, the number of jobs that the project would create, and the taxes they would pay to the local and provincial governments. All seemingly good stuff.

Then came the customary question and answer period. Normally, this would be a tame affair in a community like Timmins, where almost everyone's livelihood was linked to a mine or a supply company working for a mine. A few questions were asked about the schedule, project specifics, and the freeze wall. Nothing too probing. The company representatives were able to handle all of them quite easily, and anyone who might have had actual concerns must have kept quiet to avoid being identified as possibly not supporting the industry. This is always an issue in a small resource town where the majority of people's livelihood comes from a particular industry. To ask question means you are possibly threatening someone's livelihood, and most people do not want to fall into that camp.

Things appeared to be winding down, and the company representatives were getting ready to say, "Thank you. If you have further questions, please contact us."

But then the man in the blue jeans, heavy coat, and ball cap put up his hand.

The Echo Bay man acknowledged him.

"I have a question," he said.

"Please go ahead. Thank you."

People in the room turned to look at him.

"I want to begin by stating that the land we gather on is within the traditional territories of Matachewan First Nation, Flying Post First Nation, and Wahgoshig First Nation. This area has been used by us for generations. We have hunted, fished, and lived here for thousands of years and will for many years to come. Thank you for providing me with the opportunity to hear about your project that you call Aquarius. I want to be clear: I am not against mineral exploration and mining. I understand the land is rich with minerals and most of the people in this room make a living and support families with the jobs and business that come from the mines here. I have found some gold myself over the years and believe there is a lot more here." He moved his right arm in a sweeping motion, pointing toward the window and the land outside.

"If any of you want some help in finding more, please give me a call, and maybe we could get rich together. My nephew really wants a new snowmobile." He laughed a little, as did a few people in the audience, before continuing. "When it comes to this Aquarius project, I feel as if I need to say a few things to maybe help you understand our perspective. An Indian perspective. What I want you to understand is that when you talk of the environment, of water quality, of the health of fish, you and your experts speak as if they are something external. Something to be studied. To 'monitor the health of,' as one of you said. For First Nations Peoples, we do not see things this way. Water to us is life. It is alive. The environment is Mother Earth and what sustains us. Fish are what feeds us and nourishes our families. They all deserve our respect.

"I am not an engineer and cannot say whether your freeze wall will work. It seems kind of crazy to me if I am honest, though. Freezing the ground like that to hold back the water of such a big lake. Maybe in winter. But in summer? Crazy, if you ask me, and I worry that it will fail, as so many things that are not supposed to seem to do. What I see, when I look at this project and what you and your scientists and engineers are proposing, is risk. And that risk is my people's life and future. A future for you to mine for gold and become rich, with no benefits coming to us. Only risk. We are not part of this project, and I do not think ever will be. I know I am only one voice here in this room, but I need you to know that for too long, Indian voices have been ignored. We will not let that happen anymore. Thank you for listening to me."

The room was quiet. The company representatives looked to one another, seeing who might be prepared to respond.

The man who had spoken did not wait for an answer. This was more than twenty years ago, and he knew that a satisfactory response would not come. Not then. He just looked directly at the company management team, got up, and walked slowly out of the room and the building.

People were quiet for a few more moments before the Q & A restarted. Despite the importance of what the man had so eloquently said, it was barely acknowledged by the company representatives or their consultants. The meeting wrapped up a short time later, and people gathered their belongings to go home.

Behind me I heard a few locals comment to one another as people were getting up to leave. "Crazy old man. I am sure he is on his way back to the pub for a drink." A few others laughed at this and nodded in agreement. And there was more, but I would rather not put those words down in writing. You get the gist of where that was going.

I left that meeting on my own and drove back to the house I was staying in, which was just up the road. It was a place my employer, another one of the local mining companies, had provided for me when I had come out a few months earlier from Vancouver to work.

I remember feeling a profound sense of sadness and disappointment at how the final part of the meeting had gone down. I wish I could have gone and spoken to the man who had voiced his concerns. Found out his name. Where he lived. Asked him to tell me stories about these traditional lands and of his people.

I never got that chance, and I never saw him again. The memory of what he said, how it made me feel, how his words did not get anywhere near the respect or acknowledgement they deserved—along with the racist attitudes expressed by some in the audience—has stuck with me to this day, though. It was very wrong then, as it would be now. It was also a foreshadowing of the Indigenous empowerment and advocacy around industrial development that would explode in the years since then. As we have now seen.

Summary

Many Indigenous Peoples and communities view the land and the water of their lands as the vital parts of Mother Earth that provide them with life, identity, and connection to ancestors. Affecting those threatens their well-being. As a resource proponent, it is important to recognize that "resources" are not just things to be harvested and taken away for profit. They are part of the land on which Indigenous communities have sustained their communities for thousands of years.

Traditional Ecological Knowledge and Indigenous Knowledge represent the culmination of multiple generations of learning, experience, and knowledge gained by Indigenous Peoples about the lands, waters, ecology, wildlife, fish, and climate in which they have lived. Including TEK and IK within assessments of extractive projects is critical to understanding the real impact of projects on Indigenous Peoples.

Resource projects need to be considered in the context of their legacy and impact, not just today but seven generations beyond today. This represents a challenge to established perspectives of engineering, government permitting and regulation, and project design, but also an opportunity to assess those impacts and the rehabilitative power of nature more fully over the long term.

5

How to Engage

AFTER EDUCATING yourself and doing some self-reflection, are you ready for engagement? There are diverse approaches to how companies, businesses, and industry are engaging with Indigenous communities. There are many guides that offer advice on how to engage and strategies to consultation, and as a result, the practice on the ground is often wide-ranging and diverse.

The more prevalent issue, though, is the question of a person or a company's sincerity in the engagement they are doing. Before you read any further, ask yourself: Are you committed to engaging with authenticity? Is the company you work for sincere? What does this look like? How should this look? Indigenous culture is deeply rooted in relationality; therefore, inauthentic or insincere relationships will not be successful, and engagement will suffer.

In this chapter we are going to consider these issues and try to give you a sense of what true engagement is, how to do it, and what pitfalls to avoid. There is no perfect or formulaic way to engage. These are suggestions based on our experience of what works and where things can go wrong. As with all parts of this discussion, please remember that with the rich diversity of Indigenous cultures, histories, and practices, what is presented here are only guidelines and advice and must be adapted to align with what is most appropriate for where you are and the communities you are wanting to work with.

Before hearing from Christy on principles of effective engagement, let's begin this chapter with a story from Mike about a rare-metals project in northwestern Ontario.

Mining on the Banks of the Wabigoon-English River

A little more than twenty years ago, when I was only a few years out of university, I had a job working for an engineering and environmental consulting firm in northern Ontario. We had been retained to work on a prospective metals project in the Kenora area in the northwestern region of the province, on the banks of the English River. The Wabigoon-English River drainage is an iconic waterway that is over six hundred kilometres long. It is part of the Hudson Bay drainage basin that flows through numerous lakes on its way to the Winnipeg River.

At the time, I was the person responsible for designing and carrying out environmental baseline study programs in support of the permitting of the project and delivering a reassuring message to local community members about what was being planned by the company in the area. In this case, the primary audience was the Wabaseemoong Independent Nations (also known as White Dog) and the Asubpeeschoseewagong First Nation (also known as Grassy Narrows). Both are part of the Ojibwe First Nations band government and are signatories to Treaty 3. Treaty 3 dates back to 1871 and the time of Queen Victoria. In this agreement the signatories, including both White Dog and Grassy Narrows, gave up large tracts of land in northwestern Ontario and eastern Manitoba in exchange for territory within the Wabigoon-English River system.

It was late May when we visited the area. The company was getting ready for the start of the field season. The plan was to bring several diamond-drilling rigs into the area and begin a multi-thousand-metre drill program on their mineral claims. The goal was to confirm a possible economic deposit of rare earth metals that could potentially become a mine. The company was publicly traded on the Venture platform of the Toronto Stock Exchange and was known in the business as a junior miner. The "junior" part refers to it being an exploration company without any actual operating mines.

The CEO, who was a geologist and mining promoter, and I drove into the Grassy Narrows community from the town of Kenora in our rented Ford F-250 pickup truck. It was mid-morning in late spring, with clear blue skies and a temperature of around twelve degrees. We were travelling to the area to introduce ourselves and discuss plans that the company had for work in the area. We drove into the community and sought out the band administration offices where our meeting was to be held.

When we arrived, we parked alongside several other pickup trucks with heavy winter tires and mud from driving the melting gravel roads of the area. Armed with colourful PowerPoint presentations, geological maps, and our laminated business cards with a Toronto address, we exited our truck and went up the stairs and inside the administration offices.

Upon entering, we were greeted with a nod of acknowledgement from a young woman sitting behind a desk and speaking to someone on her phone. With her free hand, she gestured for us to take a seat in the empty metal office chairs along the wall of the foyer. We did as she indicated and waited. While we were waiting for her to finish her call, both of us looked around the room. Notices were pasted on a large corkboard, advertising events like health clinics in the community, substance abuse counselling, and minutes from the latest chief and council meeting. There were also provincial and federal government brochures sitting on the table, with the Canadian flag and the "Indian and Northern Affairs Canada" logo displayed prominently on a number of them.

The woman finished her call and asked us if she could help. After the CEO explained why we were there and who we were, she directed us to sit at a large boardroom table in the adjoining room. She said she would let the chief know we were there and just to wait patiently.

After about fifteen minutes, three members of the Grassy Narrows First Nation, led by the chief, entered the room and sat down. The chief, an older, heavy-set man in a dark-red and black jacket, sat at the head of the table. Next to him was a younger man in a blue golf shirt and a Toronto Maple Leafs baseball cap, who was introduced as the band administrator. Lastly, we were introduced to a slightly older woman wearing a heavy coat and boots that looked as if they had just been used to walk across a muddy field. She was acknowledged by the chief as the head of the environment and natural resources committee of their community.

The meeting started off in a friendly way, with talk about the weather, the ongoing spring melt, and how everyone welcomed the cold weather being behind them. As we got down to business, the chief asked why we were there. The CEO of the company explained that we were there to introduce ourselves and to discuss a drilling program that was to start in the next few weeks in the area. He talked about the target of this work being a metals deposit adjacent to the English River, a few kilometres from where we were, that he felt had the potential to be "world class." He went on to say enthusiastically that, if they were successful, this could be the start of a major new mining operation in the area—something that would bring many jobs and economic opportunities—and that he would like to discuss how his company might work together with Grassy Narrows going forward.

Note that this was in the early days of the mining industry's formal engagement with Indigenous communities, and so showing up a few weeks before starting your drill program was typical.

After his introduction, the CEO asked that I explain what the company was doing on the environmental side of this and how the work being proposed would protect the land and waters of the area. I was twenty-eight years old at the time, with an undergraduate degree in physical geography and about five years of "real" experience in the business. It was my first time in this part of Ontario, and although I believed what I was about to say, I recognize, looking back, that I had no idea what I was talking about. I did my best, knowing what I did, to explain the studies that were planned and the steps that were being taken to protect the environment. I stated with conviction—but with no real knowledge or ability to verify, other than the words of the CEO—that the company would "meet or exceed all of the regulatory standards required in their work." I explained the environmental baseline studies that had recently begun and how that would help us to know if anything in the future was altering existing conditions in the area. I spoke about wanting to share that information with Grassy Narrows if they were interested and said that I would really appreciate any input they might have. And I mentioned that we had experienced engineers involved in the design of the project who would employ the highest standards of design.

All great stuff, right?

Good project, good people, and here we were doing our job, consulting with the communities of the area. Seemed like this was going well.

Or so I thought.

It was after my outline that the head of the land, environment, and resources committee of Grassy Narrows spoke. She had not said a thing until that point. I realized afterwards that I had likely spent my entire time speaking to the chief as opposed to the whole room and barely acknowledged her presence in the way I should have. It was a mistake I would never make again.

She politely thanked us for our presentation and then asked whether mining was a safe industry and if we thought there might be a risk to her people in the future from the development of a mine near the English River—a waterway that she and her people depended on and believed was sacred.

I responded, too quickly in hindsight, that yes, I believed a mine could be built and operated in the area safely. That I worked with a group of the top engineers in the field and that I was sure a project could be designed that would protect the English River and result in real economic benefit to her people.

This is the argument that is most often used by resource companies when trying to convince Indigenous Peoples to support a project.

She nodded slowly and then removed a set of papers from an envelope on the table in front of her. It was a newspaper article, and she had made copies for each of us and passed them around. In bold black type across the top of the page was the following headline: **Los Frailes Dam Fails: 4–5 Million Cubic Meters of Toxic Tailings Slurries and Liquid Threatening Doñana National Park, a UN World Heritage Area.**

In the article was a vivid description of how a tailings dam had failed and destroyed some three hundred thousand hectares of farmland and turned the Agrio and Guadiamar Rivers red. This was complete with dramatic photos of landscapes and waterways forever altered; the story was of devastation and destruction of an otherwise pristine landscape. The owner and operator that owned and operated the mine was a Swedish-Canadian company called Boliden.

After a few minutes, which allowed all of us the opportunity to take in the main points of the article, she looked at both of us with a penetrating gaze that I can still remember some twenty-five years later and asked, "Is this what you call 'safe' mining?"

Neither of us answered, and she continued: "Your project is in our traditional territory on the banks of waters that give us our livelihood and have already been polluted in a terrible way by others—others who made claims of the *best* engineering and promises of jobs." She asked, "Do you know what has happened to our people from that? Have you seen what mercury poisoning does to someone?"

The CEO and I just looked at one another, not knowing where all this was coming from.

"This disaster," she said, pointing to the papers in front of us, "which just happened a few months ago, was under the responsibility of a Canadian mining company. A company much larger than yours with presumably many *experienced* engineers." The emphasis was on the word "experienced," which I had just used in the context of my assurances to her. "And look what has happened!"

She looked at both of us and gestured to the chief and band administrator while holding up the article. "Please tell me why I, why we, should trust anything that you or your industry says?"

For me, the air just seemed to leave the room. I attempted to provide a response of affirmations about our expertise and that what had happened there was a long way away and was a different company. That we would only employ the highest standards to protect the environment and there was no way that sort of thing could happen here. The CEO of the company joined in, thanked her for raising these issues, and assured everyone that we, as well, saw this as a tragic story. He went on to explain that our project was much different and that there was no way something like that could happen with this project.

However, the point had been made, and there was not much we could say in return at that point in time. Despite our affirmations, both of us knew that what we were saying was not going to change anyone's mind then, and it was best to just listen and take in what we had heard. The meeting ended shortly after, and we made our way back to the truck.

As we pulled away and the band office faded in view behind us, the CEO turned to me and said, "Well, that did not go very well." I just looked at him and could only nod in agreement, not knowing if I was the one who had screwed up but old enough to recognize that there was a lot more to what had just happened than what I understood at the time.

The truth is, both the CEO, who is a decent man and is still in the business today, and I went into that meeting knowing little about the history of the area or the rich culture of the people who have lived there for thousands of years. Of course, we could not answer for what had happened recently in Spain, nor could we answer for what happened in the past in the area. Had we done our proper research, though, we would have understood and been much better prepared for the context of why the Los Frailes dam failure was relevant, beyond the obvious, to the people of this area.

The Dryden Pulp Mill

Near the Grassy Narrows community, there is a pulp and paper mill that was owned by Dryden Chemicals Ltd., a subsidiary of the British multinational Reed International, in the 1960s. In this operation, Dryden had discharged effluent containing an estimated nine thousand kilograms, or nine tonnes, of mercury directly into the Wabigoon-English River system over eight years. And on multiple occasions between 1970 and 1975, when Dryden Chemicals claimed it had stopped releasing mercury, Ontario officials found levels thirty times above normal and an absence of fish for sixty-four kilometres downstream. Residents noticed strange behaviour in animals: cats stumbling in circles and salivating, and turkey vultures flying in disordered patterns.[15] Toxic levels of mercury contamination were prevalent throughout the area and still exist to this day.

A study done by Japanese researchers found that some 90 percent of the population of the Grassy Narrows and White Dog First Nations had been negatively affected by mercury poisoning.[16] Mercury is a particularly brutal element that bioaccumulates in fish and wildlife and can lead to severe human health effects and even death. And it did here, and those most affected—even now, more than fifty years later—were and are the Grassy Narrows and White Dog First Nations. The health and cultural effects continue to this day and are a deep scar on the history of industrial development in the area, the province of Ontario, and Canada.

Legacy

We refer to the Dryden story for a couple of reasons. The first is that the resource industry, and the governments that enabled it, has made some terrible decisions in the past that continue to have long-lasting negative impacts on Indigenous communities. Whether these were deliberately malicious, negligent, or simply mistakes really is neither here nor there in terms of the people who have been negatively impacted.

Further, that history affects how people perceive industry and the governments that regulate them today. To say, "Trust us, it will be different this time," is clearly not enough when there have been so many examples of how that trust may have been misplaced, and the consequences have been a legacy of real harm.

The second reason is that taking the time to know the history and understand the culture and values of a community, to the greatest extent possible, is critical to being able to even begin to develop a respectful and meaningful dialogue and relationship. In the story above, this was obviously not done to the degree to which it should have been. And that lack of knowledge put them potentially in the same column as the engineers and businessmen of Dryden Chemicals, who likely offered similar assurances to the First Nation community members of the day.

Of course, the two projects are hardly the same. But knowing what we do now, the approach to proposing future development in this area and with these communities required a much different approach and sensitivity than what was offered here.

Principles of Effective Engagement

Let's turn now to some ideas from Christy on how to engage and be successful in building meaningful and productive relationships with Indigenous Peoples.

Start Early

As a general rule, begin the development of your relationships with an Indigenous community as soon as possible—at the very beginning of a project. It should be the first call you make when entering into an area. Before anyone from the company begins work on the ground, reach out and make an introduction. A general guideline is that, at a minimum, you should begin your engagement a year in advance of when you actually need to start on a project. This will allow people to get to know you, and you can show them that you are authentic—that you truly respect the people whose traditional lands you are entering and doing business on.

Most of us have heard the adage "you only get one chance to make a first impression." Think about that from the perspective of an Indigenous community. The first step should be to engage right at the beginning and establish that you recognize their legitimate and continued presence on and authority over the land and the resources on it.

Many people ask who should they engage with. This can differ between nations; it can be the chief and council, the hereditary chief, an elders' council, holders or heads of keyohs (or houses), the lands manager, the referrals department, and/ or the band administrator. I always recommend phoning the nation to determine their engagement process. Some communities have a fully documented procedure, along with the cost for reviewing documentation and engaging. There will also be times when you must engage with multiple groups; don't assume that one group holds more power of accepting or saying yes to a project than the other.

How do you start? Start with a phone call to determine who your primary contact will be and request an introduction meeting. You can also follow up with a letter of introduction. Don't be arrogant; be humble. Be someone who will be a positive, constructive presence in their area, and try to demonstrate that right at the beginning of this relationship. I have had many comments from non-Indigenous people who state that they are nervous to call the band office; I haven't quite figured this out, as we are all human. Are they nervous that they will get the door closed on them before it's even open—a possible hard "Fuck, no"?

You cannot allow fear to impede on proper engagement. Don't procrastinate; just do it—and be sincere about it.

This can be difficult sometimes because of constrained project timelines, a desire to keep your presence in an area confidential for various reasons, or uncertainty about the future of the project. And, because of those and other examples, the approach taken in these early stages may need to be adjusted and adapted. The principle here does not change, though. To be successful from the start and to create a foundation that will hopefully build resilient and productive relationships with Indigenous communities, industry must begin that process right at the beginning—not when a permit application requires it or simply to meet the legal obligations of consultation. That is not sincere relationship building.

What is needed is for industry to adapt and reframe its thinking and practices to recognize that early, authentic engagement and relationship building are a necessary part of doing business in the modern era, especially when it comes to the rights and interests of Indigenous nations.

So, start early. As early as possible. Be sincere. And take time to get to know the community—its values, culture, and people. *Especially listen to the silence.* This may sound cliché, but you can learn a lot when you listen to the silence and pauses between conversation. Don't jump to fill that silence with noise, as this may be seen as interruption. Have patience. Active listening, which is distinct from listening to respond, is part of a good relationship, and it is a tool to help gather information about a community.

Build Trust

Trust is the foundation of every successful relationship—whether it be between a proponent and a First Nation or between two people—and it must be earned. When respect is involved, things move relatively easily and progress is possible. Without it, everything is more difficult.

And, when it comes to a history of colonialism, broken promises, cultural appropriation, government policies designed to wipe out Indigenous societies, and the harmful industrial practices of the past, there is a lot to overcome in terms of Indigenous communities having a reason to trust.

Even if you are engaging with sincerity, you still have to spend time gaining and building trust. Common sense dictates that trust is not immediate. It can take months or years to build authentic trust and true relationships. Don't devalue this time and commitment.

Some ways in which to build trust include the following:

- Communicate openly and transparently.

- Strive to cause no harm.

- Be true to your word.

- Keep track of any and all commitments, and ensure they are followed through on.

- Try never to surprise.

- Don't make false promises or commitments.

- Be willing to be wrong.

- Recognize that you don't know everything.

- Don't assume one way is the right and only way.

A lack of trust in relationships for Indigenous Peoples is a result of a long history of colonial processes, broken promises, continued marginalization and oppression, and inhumane treatment. Recognize this going into a relationship and be different. Give them a reason to trust you—but do not be surprised if it is withheld, as there are many reasons for that happening.

Ask Questions (Respectfully)

Indigenous Peoples and communities are not all the same. Too often we are painted with the same brush, erasing our diversity. A particular engagement approach used with one nation may fail with another. Assuming that a person who identifies as First Nations can speak or represent the community as a whole negates the diversity of groups, removes individuality, and presumes cultural homogeneity. The diversity of First Nations groups stretches into our approach to land and resource management, tradition, culture, economy, family structures and decision-making, politics, and capacity (to name a few).

I get a lot of proponents wanting to know who to engage as the selected representative of a community and about protocols in the community around gifting. Why gift? The answers to these questions are as diverse as our communities, and specific to each. It is perfectly acceptable and respectful to ask. Some insight on appropriate gifts can be gleaned through time well spent engaging and listening. For some communities, gifting tobacco and ribbons is appropriate, where others may ask for fresh fruit or Tim Hortons. I tend not to show up empty-handed.

Shut Up and Listen

Indigenous culture is rooted in storytelling—of spirituality and beliefs, of the past, of people, of challenges, and of hopes for the future. By nature of storytelling, a teller and an audience are both needed and become connected as a result. Storytelling can be part of relationships. So be present; listen to learn and hear, and not merely to reply and be heard. I seriously could write a whole book on the subject of active and present listening as the most important element of Indigenous engagement and relationship. I have always been told I have one mouth and two ears for a reason.

When proponents enter Indigenous communities, they need to slow down and take time to really listen. Initially, taking the time to listen and learn means you may not even get to speak about the company or the project. This is okay. As you listen, if you have the urge to speak, ask yourself if you want to speak because you love to hear your own voice, and if your comment could create harm. Ask yourself if your comment would contribute value to the conversation and the budding relationship. Count to five "Mississippis" before jumping in if you need to—give enough space in between comments so, that you are not perceived to be rude and interruptive.

Time is a colonial construct that is imposed on Indigenous communities, especially via government processes, etc. The time required to build trust, engage properly, and fully understand a project is very different than what is dictated by a permitting process.

If you are entering a community with a sense of urgency to discuss a project, you have not engaged early enough. Early engagement is about the relationship. If you had a personal invitation to the family home of a possible business associate, would you spend that whole time there with a PowerPoint presentation, talking about how you would like to set up a drill in their backyard? I highly doubt it! If this was your approach, I am sure your social calendar would become very open.

There is a tendency for many to want to just talk and say what is on their mind, to discuss their project and what they might hope to achieve in the discussion. The thing is, you can get there, but you need to listen and learn first. Ask questions and listen to the answers. Look for guidance. Find out about their community and the history of the place. Ask about their families and their kids. Get to know people as people, and respect that you are in their home on their traditional territories.

Beware of Tokenism/Filling Quotas

The definition of tokenism is "actions that are the result of pretending to give advantage to those groups in society who are often treated unfairly, in order to give the appearance of fairness."

Tokenism makes my blood boil. Please refer to the section on sincerity.

In short, do not do this when you are looking to legitimately try and address issues of promoting greater diversity and inclusion in your workforce.

There are many stories and examples of companies hiring a person from a visible minority to give the appearance of promoting a diverse workforce and to be seen as progressive in this area. The challenge comes, though, when the respect, authority, mentorship, and support is not made part of the culture and practice of a company when this person or persons are brought on to the team. The work culture remains the same, and a diverse person is asked to operate within a culture that can be hostile to them or does not offer the supports necessary to that individual's success. In this case, the intent of hiring is key in understanding whether tokenism is being perpetuated or a company is truly trying to alter their workplace culture.

Industry has a long way to go before the workforce and senior management team become reflective of the cultures and diversity within our broader society. And when it comes to the mining sector, this is particularly apparent in regard to Indigenous Peoples. To meet the goals of diversity and inclusion, consider the composition not just of the operational team but also of who is around the table at head office or on the board of directors. Equity becomes an essential tool to combat tokenism—access to resources must be the same for all, including salaries, mentorship, and networking. Only once the diversity of the communities in which industry operates is seen within the executive, board, and management of companies will the risk of tokenism be removed.

Hire an Indigenous Advisor

Until recently, the presence of an Indigenous advisor in a resource company was rare, and the likelihood was that if there was one in place, they were not very Indigenously focused.

Today, nearly every company of any size will have someone in this role, and most of their focus will be on local and regional Indigenous communities. There is good reason for this, and I cannot recommend strongly enough the value of this dedicated position in terms of creating resilience in the relationships being built. Creating this position in a company and occupying it with the right person sends a message of commitment to good relationship building between Indigenous communities and project proponents. The challenge now, of course, is that with good people in such high demand, and so necessary, there is a scarcity of qualified, aware, and experienced people to fill this role.

This is not an insurmountable issue in any way. There are plenty of academic programs that teach the basics of engagement and decolonial thought, as well as people with a sincere interest in and many examples to follow of how to engage and build relationships well. What is critical is that the person in this role exemplifies the values of the company, strives to be an ally, knows how to listen well, and recognizes their role as an ambassador for the company and the project. They must engage in a good way and not create harm.

Recognize Capacity and/or Gaps in Capacity

As I mentioned previously in this chapter, all communities are diverse, and therefore there is a range of capacity to engage on technical levels. First and foremost, it is important to understand the capacity of a nation in that respect.

In most cases, traditional use and knowledge of the territory and the land are well-known. Much of this knowledge has been passed down inherently to each generation through our DNA, and in the memories stored in our cells. This is our genetic connection to the stories, the resources, other beings, the land, and its teachings.

Having adequate capacity in natural resource or land departments can be a challenge. This is not due to the lack of knowledge but rather to the time and timelines that are imposed in a colonial referral process. Knowledge of the land, waters, and plants within a traditional territory is held within communities. It is not always shared outside of communities. Multiple referrals and engagement requests often come in from government and industries concurrently. Managing multiple referrals within the parameters of colonial timelines, with limited capacity, can be challenging. Proponents are encouraged to do their research and understand capacity constraints within Indigenous communities and offices.

Lack of funding, human resources struggles, the often rural and isolated locations of communities, and the balance of administering services within their own communities contribute additional challenges to referrals and consultation processes when required. While the Crown has the duty to consult, Indigenous communities are expected to engage and respond in good faith as part of the consultation process.

Consider the things we all take for granted in urban communities, including garbage collection; clean water; fire, police, and hospital services; recreational facilities and programs;

social services; building permits; and emergency prepared-
ness. All of the same issues and demands exist within often
isolated or remote Indigenous communities; however, there
are fewer people, decreased supports, less developed infrastructure, and less administrative capacity.

So, as a proponent entering these communities looking for
input and support relating to a new mining project, understand
the pressures, capacity constraints, and other elements that
may impact engagement before setting timelines and making requests for input. And in recognizing possible constraints,
consider what could be offered as help and support. Are there
funding or human resource issues? Have you listened? What
can you do to help, or what action can you take? Is it that a lack
of knowledge relating to your project is imposing a constraint?
And if so, what could you do to help address these issues?

The reality is that some communities are looking for financial support to help build their capacity. Some communities
will not accept financial support if they do not feel that the
relationship that is being built is sincere. By accepting money,
they may think they are somehow compromising their position or mandating a particular requirement. So, as stated
before, begin by focusing on relationships and on sincerity.

Summary

Effective engagement is critical to building meaningful relationships with Indigenous Peoples. Taking the time to understand the history, culture, beliefs and concerns of Indigenous
communities is part of the engagement process, as is being
transparent and honest. Listen, ask questions, be curious,
always be respectful and get good advice. So much seems like
common sense, but the truth is many in the resource sector

have seen consultation and engagement more as an obligation rather than opportunity to create lasting, respectful relationships. Be transparent and recognize that things are often not equal in terms of capacity or experience and, in so doing, look for ways to use your influence and resources to facilitate full participation and engagement.

6

Agreements:
How, When,
and Why

O UR NEXT discussion point is about agreements. When are they needed? What form do they take? What creates the conditions for their success? We are going to touch on these issues at a high level and try and provide some guidance on what makes for a successful agreement between an Indigenous community or organization and a resource company. This is based on many years of facilitating these and helping to negotiate both high-level Memorandums of Understanding (MOUs) all the way to complex Impact Benefit Agreements (IBAs).

These can take many different forms, and there is no intent on our part to define the right approach. The diversity among Indigenous communities is immense, and as with so many aspects of this discussion, it depends on where you are in the world, the type of project being proposed, the stage of development you are at, and, ultimately, what the community demands in terms of assurances and commitments to offer consent to a development or project going ahead.

Why Enter into an Agreement?

The reality is that legal agreements are necessary in many instances to establish principles for how a relationship is intended to work, and to allocate responsibilities and expectations and define obligations of the parties involved. Legal agreements can also reduce risk to both the Indigenous community, and the resource community. For Indigenous communities, they can outline the commitment to a variety of subjects—e.g., capacity building, communication, environmental, archaeological, and business opportunities.

Our experience is that the key to effective agreements between Indigenous communities and resource companies is to limit unnecessary complexity as much as possible, and, if feasible, leave the lawyers out of it until they are needed. This can be difficult or simple, depending on the approach, the history between the parties, and the presence or absence of trust.

Here are those resource project proponents who fear entering into agreement negotiations with Indigenous communities or organizations because they fear setting precedents and enduring severe financial burdens. Well, our advice is to be honest and upfront—explain your financial situation, and most communities that wish to enter into agreements will understand or suggest other forms of recompense.

There are times when Indigenous communities do not want to enter into any sort of formalized agreement with a resource project proponent as that could be perceived as them giving support to a project that they have not yet endorsed.

There may also be a problem with the type of industry or project being proposed. Some have used the term "sin industries" to refer to resource projects and certain elements of the resource industry. Sin industries will be different depending on each community, but they could be mining, forestry, or oil and gas. There are communities that do not want to do business with these industries. Or maybe there are parts of the community who do and others who do not. This situation is quite common and can be quite difficult to work through.

It is still very important, though, to keep trying to have dialogue and communication. The answer may be "no," as we discussed previously, but our experience has been that if proponents are honest, have integrity, show respect, and are willing to respond to concerns that are raised, then the likelihood of a firm no is reduced.

Agreements 101

There has been an evolution over the past twenty years, with various forms of legal agreements being entered into between Indigenous communities and resource companies. As mentioned earlier, these range in form from relatively simple MOUs all the way to comprehensive Impact and Benefits Agreements (IBAs). The complexity of each is dependent on a host of factors, such as the type of project, stage of development, environmental or social sensitivities and risks, or the business practices and norms of the Indigenous group being engaged with.

Given the complexity of this topic and the fact that our goal here is not to try and certify our readers as corporate counsel, we will keep this discussion at a fairly high level. We will focus more on what the intent of these agreements is, how they might be applied in different situations, when they are appropriate and when there may be a better way, and the role of the various people and professions involved in these types of discussions.

It should also be noted that the law and general practices in this area are evolving almost daily. With UNDRIP and free, prior, and informed consent being the starting point of engagement in many parts of the world now, and various jurisdictions creating legislative frameworks for implementing new laws, the nature of agreements between business and Indigenous communities/nations continues to evolve as well. And finally, we are in no way dealing with a homogenous group of communities, projects, businesses, or environments, making any broad generalizations risky. What we have tried to do here is provide a framework for looking at these issues and enough substance for readers that there is a place to start with Indigenous communities.

There are a host of resources available for those interested in exploring this subject further, as well as some highly effective legal advisors who can assist proponents in this area.

Trust: An Essential Element of a Successful Agreement

Before we go into a discussion of more formal agreements, we need to talk about trust: how it is gained, how it is lost, and how those both will determine the path that is followed in terms of any sort of legal agreement. As I think most of us know, it is very difficult to legalize what is considered good practice or honesty. We can try through agreements and contracts, but if someone wants to find a way to subvert the intent or obligations of an agreement, there are often ways, and there is no way to legitimately anticipate every issue that will come up. So, despite all the work of lawyers and the courts, there is an element of trust that is necessary in order to make all this work.

Let's start with how trust is gained. There is a saying from the Duwamish people of Western Washington that "day and night cannot dwell together." This, we would offer, is a good metaphor for trust with Indigenous Peoples when it comes to relationships with industry. Trust cannot exist unless the light of honesty, consistency, and integrity are fundamental blocks on which it is built.

Too often in history, when it comes to Indigenous Peoples, this has not been the basis on which relationships were built. Instead, as we have discussed, it has been one of darkness, duplicity, treachery, and attempts by the government to extinguish Indigenous culture. That is our starting point in many instances.

So, building trust with Indigenous communities comes with a high bar to clear and some very difficult history, much that is still recent, to overcome.

Recognizing this, when it comes to building trust in a relationship with an Indigenous community, we offer that there are a few universal truths that should apply:

- Trust is built with consistency and accountability.

- Given the history of colonization and all that came with it, trust does not come easily.

- Building trust takes time—sometimes a lot of time.

- You have to accept that because of issues beyond your control or influence, you may never be trusted.

- Building and maintaining trust requires a serious commitment from everyone involved, including senior management, the board of directors, and frontline staff.

- Trust must be earned.

From a practical perspective, a few things that can go a long way toward building trust in a relationship with an Indigenous community or communities include:

- Be upfront about as much as possible at all times.

- Try not to surprise people with new information.

- If you make a mistake, own up to it and admit fault, if it is yours to acknowledge.

- Make sure that your entire management team and frontline staff understand the importance of the relationship and the commitments you or your company have made with Indigenous communities, people, and organizations.

- Create lines of communication that are clear, direct, and with the appropriate people.

- Track carefully and follow through on every commitment your company or management team makes. If for any reason that is not possible, then identify why ahead of time and make plans to address this as soon as possible.

- Consistency in who is communicating is important. If there are changes in who within an organization is tasked with communicating or engaging in the relationship with the Indigenous community, then make sure that that is known in advance and plans are put in place to address this.

- Have a line of accountability to senior management and the board on monitoring and supporting these relationships to ensure they receive the attention they deserve.

- Create ways in which to report on progress in the relationship in terms of shared goals and objectives. Share those reports and ensure that everyone buys into and supports those objectives.

- Share relevant information in real time.

- Nurture the relationship as much as possible and offer support if it is needed.

- Make sure everyone within your team who is part of engagement and supporting these relationships have appropriate training.

There are so many sayings about trust that come to mind when writing about it in this context, such as "trust can take years to build and a moment to lose" or "a lie can travel halfway around the world while the truth is putting on its shoes."

At a most basic level, it comes down to whether the parties coming to the table with Indigenous communities or organizations are worthy of being given the benefit and gift of trust. And if they are, what they do to preserve and honour it.

Let's move now to the question of when the trust that has been given is, in turn, lost. We could just play a game of "opposites" from what is listed above to consider what would cause the loss of trust: not sharing information, surprising people, inconsistent communication, not following through on commitments, and a high turnover of people. Any one of these could cause a loss of trust, either immediately or over time. And none of those consider the more dramatic possible instances of lying, betrayal, or duplicitous behaviour—which, unfortunately, are also a part of the past and current practices of the extractive industry globally when it comes to their dealings with Indigenous Peoples.

From a slightly less obvious perspective, though, there are some more subtle mistakes that companies might make that could cause the loss of whatever trust may have been gained through other means.

Some examples of these are:

- Finding out important information third-hand or inadvert-ently. This could include corporate, project, or personnel-related information that is discovered not directly but through some other means.

- Dealing with government, other communities, organizations, or businesses in ways that are at odds with the Indigenous group in question or with Indigenous interests in general.

- Contracting or procuring goods or services from outside vendors when an Indigenous community or partner is in a position to provide the same good or service.

- Interacting inconsistently with company personnel.

News releases can also cause major problems, as there needs to be some education on how things are marketed in order to raise capital. These news releases can be detrimental to relationships if they are handled improperly. This is tricky, as many are confidential and cannot be shared prior to release.

Another common scenario is companies where manage-ment completely understands what needs to get done and how to communicate, but they have a C-suite that pushes back. A technique we have used is ensuring there is cultural sensitivity and decolonization training done at the C-suite level. This can be a hard sell, as white privilege, fragility, and defensiveness kick in.

Christy recently presented this type of training to a board, and the CEO sent her the following: "I had a very privileged upbringing, such that I was raised on the stories of greatness and the success of colonization; this is triggering emotions and primarily frustration that we were not more enlightened. We need to recast that legacy in a much more accurate light."

This became a teachable moment on how to be an ally, to integrate cultural safety in the organization and truly implement reconciliation.

Like in any important relationship, and as noted above, consistency in behaviour is what builds trust over time. For companies operating in the extractive business and for many others, building trust with Indigenous communities is a major commitment and investment in time and energy. Part of this is because of the history of colonialism and examples of governments and corporations acting in a manner that, in many cases, severely harmed the health and well-being of these same communities. And much of it is also because, until more recently, the opportunity for Indigenous Peoples to fully assert their rights was not available to them, meaning that there were opportunities for those who wanted to take advantage of the relative power imbalance that existed.

So, as a company looking to build a trustful and respectful relationship with Indigenous Peoples and communities, consider an approach that is humble, empathetic, patient, open, transparent, and consistent at all times.

Agreement Options

Having dealt with the issue of trust, we now turn our discussion to that of agreements between resource companies and Indigenous communities—what they are, how they are formed, and steps to achieving a successful outcome.

The First Step

In considering a possible agreement with an Indigenous community, the first step is to understand what it is that you are trying to accomplish.

Is it to:

* Establish general principles for working together?

* Establish protocols for how to communicate and share information?

* Establish protocols for economic matters relating to contracting, business partnerships, and procurement processes?

* Establish protocols relating to employment matters relating to hiring, training, and job postings?

* Establish protocols relating to environmental matters relating to operations, environmental protection, reporting, communication, and permitting?

* Or is it to create a comprehensive impact benefits agreement that covers all these matters plus other issues of financial contributions, governance, and dispute resolution?

May we also refer you back to Chapter 1, in which we asked how you are coming to the table. The following are just some of the types of agreements you can enter into. What we have noticed lately is that many of the Indigenous communities have their own agreements to begin dialogue—don't be afraid to ask if they have anything they want to use. We were recently awed by an experience working with an Indigenous community located in the interior of the province of BC, in the negotiation of a Memorandum of Understanding relating to a proposed mineral exploration project. The MOU had been developed and rooted in the traditional language of the Nation and based on their own existing governance structure.

You will also need to ask and determine if the Indigenous community requires capacity funding to negotiate the agreement. The general rule of thumb is to provide this, but we have had nations turn this down as well.

Memorandum of Understanding (MOU)

Our typical first step when building new relationships between resource companies and Indigenous communities is to begin an MOU or Communications Agreement. This MOU can outline the process of who to communicate with, how the community will be engaged, training and business opportunities, environmental and cultural expectations, monetary support to review referrals, and the next steps to develop a more comprehensive agreement. It can also reference employment and business opportunities. One of the most important things in *all* agreements is the preamble and to ensure that your Indigenous community is satisfied with the language. The agreement should acknowledge their rights to their traditional lands and in no way give up or allude to giving up any inherent rights or titles.

Exploration Agreements

Exploration Agreements come in all shapes and sizes; no two agreements are alike, which is due to demographics, the project, and the distinct interests of that particular Indigenous community. These agreements are entered into during the exploration of a project area. They can include commitments to employment and training, business opportunities and contracts, cultural and environmental considerations, and mitigations. At the exploration level, reclamation of areas disturbed can be supported by the communities, and there should be environmental and/or heritage monitoring while work is performed at the site.

In some agreements where trust has been developed, the monetary commitment to an Indigenous community is tied to work completed by the company. This is to ensure the project is able to continue its drilling and exploration program while also ensuring that the communities are compensated.

We have had the privilege of working with forward-thinking companies where the senior management are inclusive of all their staff, are advocates for reconciliation, and this is evident in the relationships they are developing and the partnerships that have formed. The exploration agreements that we have seen work well have a key focus on Indigenous economic reconciliation. Economic reconciliation—what does this mean or look like? In this specific case, the Indigenous communities have true ownership in the company; they have oversight in the environmental and cultural impacts of the projects; and they sit with site-level and corporate-level management to discuss project decisions. Although there may be unintentional mistakes or misinterpretations made along the way, the relationship is strong enough to move through those moments.

Comprehensive Agreement/Impact Benefits Agreement

You usually enter a more robust or bridging agreement when a project is moving from exploration to the development and operations stage. Again, the structure can take multiple forms, and it can include a level of complexity that will run many volumes and consider everything, including:

- Decision-making and governance
- Environmental protection and monitoring
- Fiduciary issues and payments to the Indigenous community
- Contracting
- Employment
- Communications
- Reporting

There are many examples of these, and the law and practices in this area continue to evolve. We would encourage proponents to engage legal counsel for this work and ensure that there is strong board-level oversight and support for obligations and commitments being made on behalf of the company.

We would like to finish this chapter with a story about an agreement that we believe is considered by all parties to be a success and that represents a path that we see as being respectful, meaningful, and productive.

Nisga'a Nation and the Red Mountain and Premier Gold Projects

Both of us have had the opportunity to work on a set of gold mining projects in the far northwest of BC near the border with Alaska. Set just outside the town of Stewart, BC, and Hyder, Alaska, the Red Mountain and Premier Gold projects represent a rebirth of the storied prospecting and mining past of this area. Now owned entirely by Ascot Resources Ltd., these projects are on track for production in the relatively near term.

Nisga'a Nation

The Nisga'a are an Indigenous nation that reside in the Nass River Valley of northwestern BC. They are an extraordinary people who have an incredibly rich culture and history that stretches back thousands of years. There are so many aspects of the Nisga'a community, culture, and history that deserve mention, but that is not for us to do. For those who are interested, please take the time to visit the Nisga'a Nation website at nisgaanation.ca.

Under the leadership of Dr. Joseph Gosnell, the Nisga'a Nation signed a landmark treaty with the Government of Canada and the Province of BC in 1998 that brought them self-government and control over their land, resources, and culture. A Companion of the Order of Canada, among many other honours, Dr. Gosnell sadly passed in August 2020, but his legacy lives on with his people, and we are lucky to have gotten to know at least a few of them.

The Nisga'a Lisims Government at the time of this writing is led by President Eva Clayton and her executive team. Under this strong and forward-looking leadership, the Nisga'a are known to have been at the forefront of economic development, partnerships, and bringing positive change to their communities.

The Nisga'a Nation territory is a long way from the metropolis of Vancouver and other commercial centres. Here, massive fish-bearing rivers fed by large glaciers stretch to the horizon; mountains reach to over eight thousand feet high; the Pacific Ocean is to the west; and there is a bounty of wildlife, flora and fauna, and spectacular landscapes that could fill years of *National Geographic* magazines. And the culture, art, and strength of the Nisga'a people reflect the place in which they live.

Red Mountain

It was in this area that, in 2014, a company called IDM Mining Ltd. was formed around a project known as Red Mountain. A prospective underground gold mine had been discovered back in the 1980s, and this resource was envisaged as the next gold mine to be built in the province. The project went through a full provincial and federal environmental assessment, and it received approval from both levels of government in 2019.

It was also around this same time that IDM was taken over by Ascot Resources Ltd., and Red Mountain was combined into a portfolio of development projects, all in the same area surrounding Stewart and within Nisga'a territory. These projects are going through the final operations permitting phase at the time of writing and are expected to begin development and operations in the near term.

First Call and Agreements

When Mike and Rob McLeod, the cofounders of IDM, acquired the Red Mountain project from Seabridge Gold, the very first call they made was to the leaders of the Nisga'a Lisims Government. That old saying that "you only get one chance to make a first impression" very much applies here. Both Rob and Mike recognized that the Nisga'a were the authority on these lands and that we had to show our respect right from the beginning. For proponents looking at projects in Indigenous territories, we would highly recommend this approach. It matters. And it is the first step in working to build strong relationships.

The management and team at IDM developed a deep and meaningful relationship with the leadership and many members of the Nisga'a Nation over several years. Through employment at the project, negotiation of an exploration agreement, and collaborative work through the provincial and federal environmental assessment process, a positive working relationship and friendships were formed. This work culminated in the signing of a comprehensive Impact Benefits Agreement (IBA) in 2020, with both IDM and the new owners, Ascot, in attendance.

Ascot has gone on to expand on this IBA and include it in their projects in Nisga'a territory, and things are reportedly working reasonably well. Christy has been a key part of advising the senior management team through this, and her considerable knowledge, experience, and skill in developing resilient relationships have been invaluable to the management teams.

Trust, Transparency, and Facebook

The last part of this story is something we wanted to tell readers about because it combines so much of what we have been discussing up until now in this book, along with the modern twist of social media.

As part of IDM's overall community and Indigenous engagement efforts, meetings were held with elected leaders and their legal counsel on a regular basis. This began right at the start and carried on through the provincial and federal environmental assessment process. IDM had a policy that they would provide all permit and licence materials to the Nisga'a and their consultants as needed *before* submitting them to the traditional regulatory authorities and governments. This was done as a sign of respect to them and was always followed.

For the most part, all of this went well. Issues were worked through as they arose and in a reasonable time frame. It was not that there was always agreement, as there were vigorous debates over key issues, and those took time and effort to resolve. The key, though, was that a path could always be found that allowed the discussion and project to move forward. Legal counsel was used only sparingly, and executive management on both sides remained deeply involved at all stages.

But why was the management at IDM trusted, and how has that trust remained? Part of it was the respect that IDM management showed from the beginning. The second factor was that they followed through on commitments that had been made. The third was clear recognition of prior and informed consent, which was evidenced in the way permitting and regulatory matters were always discussed with Nisga'a leadership or their counsel in advance. The final part is something that was apparent in the often-warm receptions that IDM was given in Nisga'a communities and the positive relationships that were able to form. It was not something that was necessarily planned, and the outcome was fascinating.

The Red Mountain project included a fairly large underground and surface mineral exploration program. This site sits at an elevation of over five thousand feet in an area that is between two major glaciers called the Cambria Icefield. To say it is spectacular would be an understatement. Nestled into the mountainside was an exploration camp that could house up to sixty people and included a full kitchen, washrooms, and sleeping facilities.

A mandate from the beginning was to actively recruit and maximize employment of Nisga'a members at Red Mountain. Collaboration occurred with our major suppliers, like Matrix and More Core Diamond Drilling, among others, to support the training and employment of Nisga'a members. Over several years, dozens of Nisga'a members were gainfully employed, and they gained valuable transferable skills and earned family-supporting wages. There were some individual success stories that were truly life-affirming, and we give credit to the IDM team for creating an atmosphere of respect and support that allowed these young men and women to do so well.

One aspect of this that was not anticipated was the power of social media in communicating the stories of Red Mountain and the work there on an ongoing basis back to the Nisga'a communities. This was not something that, at a corporate level, IDM had any involvement in. It was the spontaneous postings of these Nisga'a members living and doing their work that were being seen by other members of their community, including elders and elected leaders, every day.

The picturesque nature of the Red Mountain area helped, we think, because most of the posts were spectacular in terms of scenery. But we think the key was that the stories being told by Nisga'a members through pictures and words were totally spontaneous, unfiltered, and uninfluenced by the company. They were people showing their pride in their work and what they were doing. Community members, leaders, and elders saw this and could experience those successes along with them. There is no corporate control in this. This was real life, with real people telling their stories.

What we realized in seeing this was how influential the transparency of social media can be in a setting such as this. If

IDM had been running a shoddy operation, harming the environment or not taking health and safety seriously, there would be no way to control that information. Instead of something negative, what those who viewed the numerous posts from members of their own community saw were images of pride; hard work; and a clean, safe, professional operation. And for a people who have long fought to overcome a history of colonialism, residential schools, and a myriad of social issues, seeing their own young people working, having success, and being proud of what they were doing was a powerful message.

Summary

This chapter has been about agreements. In many ways, though, it could just as easily be a chapter about how to build trust. Because the need for and complexity of legal agreements are often inversely proportional to the amount of trust the exists within a given relationship. We believe there are relatively straightforward legal agreements and/or memorandums of understanding that can be used to clarify and establish key characteristics of the relationship between Indigenous communities and resource companies. These can be valuable in confirming the nature of the relationship between the parties. As projects get larger and more complex, the need for more sophisticated agreements increases. There are good precedents to follow in this, and what is critical is to always recognize that with all effective agreements their foundation is built on the basis of trust, accountability, and the commitment of the parties.

7

Allyship and the
Opportunity
of Indigenomics

S WE look forward, let's consider both the foundation of what we are trying to do and the opportunities that can arise if we get it right.

Being an ally is about taking a significant step beyond engagement and consultation. It is a powerfully positive idea and one that we believe could form the basis for true reconciliation and resilient relationship building. It links the discovery, extraction, and use of materials from the land with Indigenous self-determination, success, and community well-being. It is about saying that if there is support and consent to advance a particular resource project, then we should combine strengths, join worlds, weave two worlds together, and ensure more equitable sharing of the economic benefits, environmentally and socially sustainable developments, and stronger and more resilient communities.

As we have discussed, the resource industry—which involves extraction of the earth's resources as a business—can often be found at the centre of the discussion and debate around Indigenous interests and rights globally. Much of the land, the waters, and all that lived upon or in them in North America and globally is or was once under the stewardship of Indigenous Peoples. And those resources both below and above the ground have been what sustained their people. And, on that basis, those same people, those same communities, those Indigenous nations should all have a say in what happens to those resources today and be partners in their extraction and use, if that is to occur.

The position we take is that through our examination of history, of rights, of fairness, and of the future, there is a distinct opportunity for those involved with the resource industry to be a positive and constructive influence on the journey toward reconciliation. And with that will come the opportunity for the sustainable and shared development of the earth's natural resources. It represents an opportunity for us to reposition and reframe the business of the entire resource sector globally to one that is not only done in partnership with Indigenous Peoples but is driven forward by them in a sustainable way.

As an example, consider the following, which is from a news release by TDG Gold Corp. on July 5, 2021:

- Furthermore, TDG wishes to take this opportunity to acknowledge clearly and without any ambiguity that we acknowledge the historical role the natural resource sector has played in the setting of colonial priorities, policies and conduct by established institutions including itself and that has forever impacted Indigenous Peoples. Change is required; and that requires agents of change. It also requires allyship.

- Many of us have some idea of what societal healing looks like and perhaps where we'd like to go with our ideas but, sometimes, we have an unclear sense of how to get there. Some of us are impatient, wishing for a clear timeline to healing. Some of us are terrified, dipping our toe into water[,] never wanting to offend. TDG's path to reconciliation includes wanting to educate ourselves while helping others, acknowledging our shortcomings.

- As active participants in reconciliation, we have a court-mandated path that has been lit for us. Let's not make the same mistakes with our healing policies and desires. We have to change our own behaviours and be mindful that saviors are not needed—solidarity is. It's time to slow ourselves down, listen to and learn from our Indigenous communities[,] following their path to the light [and] assisting when requested.

- TDG commits to continually work on our relationships and allyships with the Indigenous communities with whom we work.

The Opportunity Before Us

The next part of our discussion is both a challenge and an inspiration to write about—the challenge being the gulf between where we are today and where things could be, and the inspiration being the truly extraordinary timing and opportunities that exist today and into the future.

There is easily accessible economic data available about the size and makeup of industries, the economic value of various activities, and information on the proximity of Indigenous communities to natural resources like minerals, oil, gas, forests, and water. Each of these sectors of the resource economy have their own value chains, ways of doing business, and leaders who are moving things forward. They also have some backward-looking, non-progressive leaders and companies who have the potential to slow things down for their own reasons or because of their ignorance. That, unfortunately, is the world we are in—and likely always will be. There are always those trying to do good and build good relationships, and those working solely for their own benefit.

From an Indigenous perspective, it could not be simpler in terms of connecting the dots between proximity, scale, and the scope of economic opportunity associated with the sustainable development of these natural resources. The issue is that the opportunity for Indigenous communities, nations, and people is, in essence, limitless. The size and scope of these industries, many of which have been around for a long time and are well-established globally, is massive. The discovery, extraction, processing, transportation, trading, and manufacturing associated with the resource sector is a highly integrated and sophisticated market that involves hundreds of thousands of people and businesses, as well as most of the countries in the world. And with that, defining how we get from where we are today in terms of a small presence of Indigenous businesses and people engaged in the industry to what the future could be is very much open to multiple scenarios, ideas, and points of view.

Take minerals, for example. The global mining and minerals market is expected to reach a value of USD$2.4 trillion in 2025, with a compound annual growth rate (CAGR) of 7 percent.[17] Further, as noted by the Editorial Board of Mineral Choices, "population growth, urbanisation, and consumerism, coupled with the urgent need to decarbonize, [have] triggered a dramatic surge in the demand for minerals."[18]

Similarly, for liquified natural gas (LNG), there are hundreds of billions of dollars being invested in Canada and globally to produce an alternative to more carbon-intensive fuels. Sustainable forest management and value-added wood products also represent an ongoing area of innovation and opportunity.

Renewable energy sources—such as hydroelectric, tidal power, geothermal, solar, and wind—continue to grow and innovate as viable alternatives to our more traditional fuel sources for electricity and heat. After staying flat in 2020, global power sector investment is set to increase by around 5 percent in 2021 to more than USD$820 billion. Renewables dominate investment in new power generation and are expected to account for 70 percent of 2021's total of USD$530 billion spent on all new-generation capacity.[19]

Finally, oil and gas development—although this is something many countries are looking to wean themselves off of, due to legitimate concerns over rising carbon levels in the atmosphere and climate change—remains a massive multi-trillion-dollar industry globally.

And opportunity exists through the value chain of these industries—from professional services, including science and engineering, to equipment and supplies, to transportation, human resources, and administration. The number of businesses and entire industries that are connected to the resource sector is extraordinary. For example, it is estimated that for every direct job in a mining operation, there are upward of three additional jobs that come from the services and suppliers that contract with it.

So, as we started with, the inspiration is the scale and scope of the opportunities that are associated with the development and operation of resource projects with and by Indigenous Peoples, communities, and businesses. The challenge is how best to take advantage of that, given inherent biases that favour more traditional resource companies, the lower relative levels of investment history and experience, limited capital availability, and less experience within Indigenous communities with how to operate successfully in the global resource market.

As we have noted before, this is where we believe the resource industry has a distinct and very important role to play in helping to bridge the gaps between inspiration, challenges, and opportunities.

An Example from a Western Canadian Mineral Exploration Project (Slightly Fictionalized)

"Robert, we have a great opportunity for the community to consider," said the exploration manager of a mid-tier, publicly traded mining company from Toronto.

Let's call him EM for short.

"Well, that sounds great," said Robert (not his actual name), who is the economic development manager for the First Nation whose land the mineral exploration project is located on. "Tell me about it."

"Well, as a result of our recent successes, we need to build a new camp up at the gold property we have been speaking with you about," EM replied. "The camp will be a fairly good size, with room to handle initially up to a hundred people. We will have a core cutting facility, a new kitchen, new offices, a workout gym, and all the extras that are needed to make it a place where people will enjoy living and working. We will also need to have help running the camp, and a supply of catering services, first aid, and site maintenance and cleaning. We are looking to have this all bid externally and expect this to be a sizable seven-figure contract. We think this would be a great opportunity for the nation to get into the camp services business. And we would really love for you and the team to be involved in all or some of this."

"Okay. Thanks for telling me all this," said Robert, with some tentativeness in his voice. "What is your timing for this work?"

"Well, as per our agreement, I am bringing this to you one week in advance of when the request for proposals, or RFPs, will be sent out more broadly to other commercial firms in the province. Our intent is to allow, say, three weeks to bid on the project, and then we would like to award within two weeks after that. Assuming we have workable proposals," EM continued. "And then we can get going!"

"And when do you want to have everything up and running in this new camp?" Robert asked.

"The goal is to have everything up and running by October 15," said EM. "That is four months from now, with the first crews arriving that week to work." EM looked across the room at Robert, with a smile that you would expect from someone who had just given you a present—one the giver believes that you should really like. "What do you think?"

There was a long pause as Robert took some time to ponder what had been said. He was not so sure he liked what he had been "given." "Well, as I said, I think it sounds interesting. But I am not sure we can do anything in that kind of timeline. Even with the extra week. This is a major contract and will require a significant commitment of time and resources from me and others to put together in a competitive bid. It will also require the support of the chief and council if we are bidding on something over a million dollars. Those are our rules. They are not scheduled to meet again for another four weeks. We just had a council meeting last night, and I believe the chief is planning to take her granddaughter back east for a few weeks." Robert concluded by stating, "I do not see any way that we can make all that happen in the timeline you have outlined."

Now there was a pause on the other side of the line as EM contemplated how to respond. On the one hand, he understood what Robert was saying and recognized that the timeline they had developed would not work for the nation. They had two apparent choices at that moment. One was to proceed ahead and see if there would be some way to have the nation partner up with one of the other bidders to put in a quote for the project. The other was to extend the timeline and work with the community to build up their ability to put in a full bid on the project. The challenge with that was that it would put the entire project at risk and threaten their field programs and what had been promised to senior management, the board of directors, and their shareholders.

As well, the company that EM works with has an agreement in place with the First Nation. And that agreement has a series of commitments for the company to support the development of businesses within the nation and have a procurement policy that gives preference to bids that are from businesses led by First Nations.

So, what should the exploration manager do? This, we would offer, would be an interesting exercise to do with your senior and operations management teams—to see how people would assess this situation and respond. Would the exploration manager use some creativity, empathy, and awareness of what was happening behind the words of this conversation and try to come up with a workable solution that would allow the First Nation to be meaningfully involved in this proposal and contract discussion? Or would their priority be the need to have the new camp up and running on time and, rather than looking for other ideas about how to make this work, focus only on meeting the bare requirements of their agreement? Or are there some other options that could be considered?

We would really encourage you to think about this and put yourself in the position of EM. How would you respond? And think about, as you did in Chapter 1, your own biases and levels of real commitment to being an ally of Indigenous Peoples.

Just for fun, let's outline a couple of scenarios that might come from a discussion or situation such as this.

Scenario One

In the first scenario, EM takes the position that the most important metric for the company and himself is the success of the field program he is responsible for. And that it starts on time. To do that, he must have the camp up and running by October 15, or everything will be in jeopardy with winter coming and so forth. So, following the letter of his company's agreement with the First Nation, he provides the RFP to them a week in advance of the other bidders but leaves everything else the same.

As expected, the First Nation does not have the resources or capacity to make a bid for a several-million-dollar new camp build and operations contract in the time available to them. So, they decline to bid. In explaining this outcome to senior management, EM says that he tried, had multiple conversions with the nation, gave the RFP in advance as per their agreement, but that they still declined to bid. Senior management takes this at face value, agrees to award the contract to the lowest bidder, and suggests to EM that he makes sure the First Nation is made aware of who the successful bidder is and what the job opportunities might be.

There is no extra effort made, as the company and management teams have other priorities to address.

Scenario Two

In this scenario, EM has a more enlightened world view and recognizes that it is not reasonable to expect a First Nation with no prior formal experience in building or operating work camps to put forward a successful bid for a multimillion-dollar project like this in the time available to them. So, he takes a different tactic and approaches it as an opportunity to build capacity and create the foundation for new business development in the future.

The first thing he does is discuss his idea with Robert, the economic development coordinator with the nation, to ensure that everyone is on board. With that in hand, he contacts all the companies that are considering bidding on the project and lets them know the timing and process for the RFP. He advises them that in addition to the evaluation criteria relating to price, performance, and safety, a significant consideration will be their experience and demonstrated track record of working with Indigenous communities in a positive way. He also explains that explicit in the contract, if they are successful, will be a timeline for the eventual graduation of the work and operations of the camp to be under the direction and ultimate control of their First Nation partners. He is explicit that, as the successful bidder, they will be responsible for helping to build the capacity, knowledge, and understanding of the work with members of the First Nation—the ultimate goal of this being that they become the owners and operators.

In so doing, to be successful, the bidder will need to show how they will work with the nation to build an Indigenous-owned and -led industrial camp services business, with the first customer being the EM's company. The structure of that business and whether the bidder is involved going forward will be up to them to sort out.

The result of this approach is that the EM gets to have his new camp on time; the relationship with the First Nation they are working with improves in a number of important ways; the senior management of EM's company are happy because all of their, the board's, and the shareholders' objectives are being met; and there is now a positive legacy from this that will, hopefully, last far beyond the time of this one project as this new company bids on other projects in the region and grows.

Outcomes

The scenarios above are real, and we have seen variations on them many times.

On the one hand, you have managers and operators who come with a world view that companies should, if they are forced to, give Indigenous Peoples and businesses some advantage in bidding on projects and securing employment. The cost of doing business these days, some might say.

However, that in and of itself is rarely enough to see actual progress being made and real benefits flowing to the nations, other than possibly more passive related proceeds like royalties or a small percentage of contract values—things that will end when the project ends.

However, there are other examples where there are more enlightened, aware, and experienced managers and operators who recognize that the presence of an opportunity does not mean it can be taken advantage of if the capacity, experience, people, time, or knowledge is not there. And the lack of those things should not mean that Indigenous businesses or communities should be excluded from the opportunities that are taking place within their territory because of timelines imposed on them by those from the outside.

So, that enlightened and experienced group assesses the situation and understands that they have an explicit role and responsibility to help create the conditions for the nation to be successful. This does not mean giving things away or not conducting a proposal process openly and transparently. It means recognizing that if the intent is to build capacity, to create a deeper relationship, and to truly be an ally with Indigenous Peoples, then leading non-Indigenous companies need to be thoughtful, creative, and committed to generating long-term economic opportunities that are inclusive and that leave a legacy that benefits future generations.

That is a good outcome and true allyship with Indigenous Peoples.

Case Studies

In this next section, we refer to and provide commentary on several case studies of Indigenous and non-Indigenous businesses and communities working together on resource projects. These examples are drawn from across Canada and from all the major parts of the resource sector, including mining, forestry, energy, seafood, and transportation. They have been chosen to try and represent the wide-ranging and dynamic nature of what is taking place today. It is an exciting time, and if these cases are any indication of the future, which we believe they are, there will be many more examples to consider in the months and years ahead.

Case Study One: Sale of Ridley Terminals Inc. (Prince Rupert, BC)

Ridley Terminals (RTI) is a marine bulk-export facility located in northwestern BC. Established in 1983, the initial construction of Ridley Terminals was a joint venture between the federal government and Federal Commerce & Navigation, in support of coal developments in northeast British Columbia. In 1991, the federal government became sole owner of the terminal and ran it as a crown corporation until its sale in late 2019.

RTI is a key export point for metallurgical and thermal coal, petroleum coke, and liquefied petroleum gas from BC and Alberta to Asia, and it operates seven days a week, twenty-four hours a day. The company employs approximately 150 people and is a major part of the northern economy of the province and the Pacific Gateway.

The terminal sits within the traditional territories the Lax Kw'alaams Band and the Metlakatla First Nation. The Lax Kw'alaams community is located approximately twenty kilometres north of Prince Rupert. The Lax Kw'alaams Band is members of the Nine Tribes of the Coast Tsimshian. The name Lax Kw'alaams derives from Laxłgu'alaams, which means "place of the wild roses" in Sm'algyax, the language of the Coast Tsm'syen (Tsimshian).

The Metlakatla First Nation village is located five kilometres north of Prince Rupert, on an ancient site that has been occupied for thousands of years. The Metlakatla are also members of the Nine Tribes of the Coast Tsimshian. Metlakatla means "saltwater passage" in Sm'algyax, the language of the Coast Ts'msyen (Tsimshian).

SALE: In 2019, Ridley ended its status as a crown corporation with the sale of 90 percent of the corporation to two private US equity firms, Riverstone Holdings LLC and AMCI Group, for CAD$350 million. The remaining 10 percent was transferred to a limited partnership owned by the Lax Kw'alaams Band and Metlakatla First Nation.

CURRENT STATUS: The terminal is reportedly doing well, and the partnership between Riverstone, AMCI, the Lax Kw'alaams Band, and Metlakatla First Nation appears to be solid. There is tremendous opportunity for RTI to continue to diversify into new markets and be an important part of Canada's export infrastructure to overseas markets.

OUR THOUGHTS: I (Mike) served as chair of the board of Ridley Terminals during the two-year-plus-long sale process, from 2017 to the end of 2019. Having been appointed by the minister of transport and charged with ensuring that the sale process went smoothly from a board- and RTI-operations perspective,

I think the outcome here was positive for several key reasons. First, the value the Government of Canada received for the 90 percent was meaningful and a benefit to all Canadians. Second, the sale occurred in a relatively seamless fashion, with broad support of both the existing customers and the community. And finally, and I think in many ways most importantly, it was carried out in a way that was fully respectful and to the benefit of the Indigenous Peoples of the area, whose presence goes back many thousands of years. The transfer of a meaningful ownership of a major public infrastructure facility to the Lax Kw'alaams and Metlakatla will hopefully result in long-term, sustainable economic benefits coming to their communities.

I (Christy) agree with Mike that there are benefits from this agreement. Although this is a good example of the beginning of economic reconciliation, Ridley Terminal has been doing business at this location for thirty-five years, and they have a lot of catching up to do.

Case Study Two: Acquisition of Clearwater Seafoods by Premium Brand Holdings and a coalition of Mi'kmaq First Nations

On January 25, 2021, Premium Brands Holdings Corporation (Premium Brands) and a coalition of Mi'kmaq First Nations announced the successful completion of the acquisition of Clearwater Seafoods Incorporated (Clearwater). Premium Brands and the coalition of Mi'kmaq First Nations, through a subsidiary owned 50 percent by each, acquired all of the issued and outstanding common shares of Clearwater in a transaction valued at approximately $1 billion, including debt.

CLEARWATER: Clearwater is one of North America's largest vertically integrated seafood companies and the largest holder of shellfish licences and quotas in Canada. It is recognized globally for its superior quality, food safety, diversity of species, and reliable worldwide delivery of premium wild, eco-certified seafood, including scallops, lobster, clams, cold-water shrimp, langoustine, whelk, and crab. Since its founding in 1976, Clearwater has invested in science, communities, people, and technological innovation, as well as resource management to sustain and grow its seafood resource. This commitment has allowed it to remain a leader in the global seafood market and in sustainable seafood excellence.

MI'KMAQ FIRST NATIONS: FNC Holdings is a new legal entity formed for the purpose of this investment in Clearwater. FNC Holdings was legally formed by Membertou and Miawpukek First Nations, who took a leading role in the Clearwater acquisition.

According to a November 20, 2020, press release regarding the transaction,

> Given the importance of this investment opportunity to the future prosperity of Mi'kmaq communities, all First Nations in Nova Scotia, along with Miawpukek First Nation from Newfoundland and Labrador, were provided the opportunity to participate in the collective investment.
>
> The collective investment of the First Nations in Clearwater represents the single largest investment in the seafood industry by any Indigenous group in Canada. Commercial investments in the seafood sector are a strategic investment to advance the prosperity of First Nations communities and position First Nations as equal participants in the commercial economy. In addition to ongoing advancement in the implementation of treaty rights, this historic commercial investment will benefit Mi'kmaq communities in Nova Scotia and Newfoundland and Labrador for generations to come.

PREMIUM BRANDS: Based in BC, Premium Brands owns a broad range of leading specialty food manufacturing and differentiated food distribution businesses, with operations in British Columbia, Alberta, Saskatchewan, Manitoba, Ontario, Quebec, and Nova Scotia, as well as in Arizona, Minnesota, Mississippi, Nevada, Ohio, and Washington. Servicing over twenty-two thousand customers, the company and its family of brands and businesses includes dozens of well-known and specialty brands.

OUR THOUGHTS: What is not to like about this deal? Equal partnership. Significant value. Major presence in a critical industry in the country. An example of how Indigenous businesses can lead in major segments of the global economy. This transaction, we believe, points to a very bright future for Indigenous businesses and entrepreneurs.

This is powerful, and we expect to see more of these partnerships in the future as more and more Indigenous communities develop stronger roles in the economy. What makes this even more grounded in Indigenous ways is the fact that these communities are taking a leadership position in developing major economic benefit for their communities via a method and an industry that has been a part of their history for thousands of years.

Case Study Three: Forestry

There are two examples from the forest sector that we believe will be of interest to our readers, and both are important for different reasons.

Agoke Development Corporation

In northwestern Ontario, near the municipality of Greenstone, three First Nations are working together to increase

Indigenous participation and ownership in the forest industry. The First Nations—Aroland, Eabametoong, and Marten Falls—jointly own the Agoke Development Corporation (Agoke), which manages the Ogoki Forest. The Ogoki Forest is located within the three First Nations' traditional lands, but a sawmill held the Sustainable Forest Licence (SFL) for the area until 2008, when it went bankrupt. The licence then reverted back to the Crown.

In March 2015 the three First Nations signed a cooperation agreement to work together on forest management and business ventures. This led to the establishment of the Agoke Development Limited Partnership (ADLP), which was incorporated in September 2015. The ADLP is equally owned by all three First Nations, and it was designed as a vehicle to pursue forest management and keep business separate from politics.

Over the following three years, according to a report by Wood Business and Agoke, the ADLP went through the steps of developing a business plan and consulting with the Ontario Ministry of Northern Development, Mines, Natural Resources and Forestry for a forest licence and negotiating a joint venture agreement with a local sawmill to take the logs. The MNR signed a two-year interim forest resource licence with Agoke, and their business moved forward.

The project has reportedly increased employment in the mill to be 80 percent Indigenous, and it has been a boost to the local economies. The joint venture agreement also stipulated the promotion of apprenticeship training within the sawmill, with a preference for Indigenous Peoples to access these opportunities. In 2019 Agoke and Nakina Lumber delivered Level 1 apprenticeship training for ten incumbent workers for millwright and electrician careers.

According to a January 6, 2021, report by Canadian Forest Industries (CFI), looking ahead, Agoke's main goal is to get a long-term licence from the MNR. Currently, the organization has an interim licence, which will last until 2022. But this makes it difficult to get financing for equipment that needs to be used for five to seven years.

Huumiis Ventures and Western Forest Products

On May 3, 2021, Huumiis Ventures Limited Partnership (Huumiis), which is beneficially owned by the Huu-ay-aht First Nations (Huu-ay-aht) and Western Forest Products Inc. (Western), announced the completion of Huumiis's acquisition of an incremental 28 percent ownership interest in TFL 44 Limited Partnership (TFL 44 LP) and TFL 44 LP's general partner, TFL 44 General Partner Inc. (TFL 44 GP) from Western, for CAD$22.4 million. With the completion of this transaction, Huumiis now owns a 35 percent interest in TFL 44 LP and TFL 44 GP, with Western owning the remaining 65 percent.

As described in the May 3 release:

> The shared vision of Huumiis, Huu-ay-aht, and Western includes a framework for opportunities for increased participation of area First Nations through tenure ownership, training, employment and business opportunities, sustained domestic manufacturing, integrated resource management planning, marketing, and value-added product innovation. TFL 44 First Nations also sit on an advisory committee to the TFL 44 GP board. There is a shared vision for strong environmental stewardship, which will be enhanced by the collective implementation of the Huu-ay-aht-led Hišuk ma c'awak Integrated Resource Management Plan (IRMP).
>
> The closing of this stage of the transaction paves the way for the next stage—the acquisition of a further 16 percent ownership interest in TFL 44 LP and TFL 44 GP by Huumiis from Western, which would bring Huumiis's ownership

interest to 51 percent in both. This next stage is anticipated to close in the first quarter of 2023, subject to customary closing conditions, including approval by the Provincial Government of BC and a further vote by Huu-ay-aht citizens at a people's assembly.[20]

ABOUT HUU-AY-AHT FIRST NATIONS AND HUUMIIS VENTURES LIMITED PARTNERSHIP: Huu-ay-aht First Nations is an Indigenous community located on the west coast of Vancouver Island. It is a part of the Nuu-chah-nulth Nation, formerly called the Nootka.

ABOUT WESTERN FOREST PRODUCTS INC.: Western is an integrated forest products company that is building a margin-focused log and lumber business to compete successfully in global softwood markets. With operations and employees located primarily on the coast of BC and Washington State, Western is a premier supplier of high-value specialty forest products.

OUR THOUGHTS: In researching examples from the forest sector and looking at the examples provided here, one thing that was apparent right away was how recent many of the stories of partnerships between forest companies and Indigenous communities were. This suggests that much of this is happening in real time, and it is likely there will be many more stories like this in the months and years ahead.

These two case studies have both similarities and differences. With Huumiss Ventures and Western Forest Products, what stands out is the sophistication of the deal that was announced and how ownership of the respective parties will evolve over a relatively short period of time—with Huumiis Ventures advancing to a 51 percent stake in the venture and

Western becoming the minority partner. This is significant in many ways, because as a business, if you own 51 percent, then you are the decision-maker on key issues. Western has a significant stake and will bring their expertise, financial resources, and capacity to the table, but they have ceded control, and it will be Huumiis that will be making the decisions on fundamental issues on their traditional lands.

We have mixed views on the Agoke Development story. On one level, it is a great story of three First Nations communities working together and creating a viable business. That takes a lot of work, and the leadership of these communities deserve recognition for this.

What we find difficult in this, though, is the approach of the Ontario Ministry of Natural Resources in terms of them providing only interim forest licences to Agoke. Two years is not enough time for any business to operate successfully and plan ahead. Having the threat hanging over them that the licence might not be renewed makes it almost impossible to get financing, hire staff, plan, or do the things a business needs to do to prepare for the future. The approach of the MNR seems paternalistic, and it follows outdated colonial practices that treat Indigenous Peoples not as equals but as second-class citizens.

Case Study Four: The Haisla Nation and LNG Canada

This is a study of the largest ever industrial investment in Canada done with the support of and in partnership with local Indigenous communities. Located in northwestern BC, Canada, the LNG Canada joint venture is building a liquefied natural gas (LNG) export facility in the town of Kitimat. LNG Canada is a joint venture comprised of Royal Dutch Shell plc, PETRONAS, PetroChina Company Limited, Mitsubishi Corporation, and Korea Gas Corporation.[21]

LNG Canada received its Environmental Assessment certificate from the Province of BC and Government of Canada in June 2015 and announced a Final Investment Decision to build the LNG export facility in Kitimat, in the traditional territory of the Haisla Nation on October 1, 2018.

The LNG plant and CGL pipeline will together employ approximately ten thousand people at peak construction with up to nine hundred people at the plant during the operations of the first phase. The total investment by the project partners in LNG Canada is estimated at CAD$40 billion.[22]

In addition to the export facility, TransCanada Corporation is in the process of building the 670-kilometre Coastal GasLink (CGL) pipeline that will connect natural gas from northeastern BC to the LNG Canada export plant in Kitimat. TransCanada has reportedly signed project agreements with all twenty elected First Nations governments along the approved pipeline route.[23] We acknowledge in this, however, that not all members of the Nations along the CGL route are supportive of the agreements made with TransCanada, and this remains an active discussion for some members of these communities.

ABOUT THE HAISLA FIRST NATION: The Xa'is'la or Haisla, meaning "*dwellers downriver*," have occupied lands of the area in which the LNG Canada project is taking place for over nine thousand years. Today, the Haisla people are centred on Kitamaat Village. Home to about half of the 1,700 Haisla, Kitamaat Village sits at the head of the Douglas Channel in BCs. The rest of the Haisla live elsewhere in the region or in Greater Vancouver.

Today's Haisla Nation is an amalgamation of two historic bands—the Kitamaat of the Douglas and Devastation channels and the Kitlope of the upper Princess Royal channel and

Gardner canal. Neighbouring nations include the Heiltsuk and Wuikinuxv bands of the Coast Tsimshian peoples.

Further information on the rich history, culture and leadership of the Haisla Nation can be viewed on their website athaisla.ca.

BENEFITS: It is not for us to define what the benefits have been for the Haisla or other First Nations in the region of the LNG Canada project. However, we can listen to and read what is stated publicly by the Haisla, other First Nation leaders, community members,[24] and the leadership of the LNG Canada partners. From that, and in considering statistics from government sources on such measures as employment, business activity and investment, it is clear the socioeconomic contributions of this project have been transformative in this region and that LNG Canada has made a serious commitment to ensuring that benefits from the project flow to local and Indigenous communities. As reported by LNG Canada, as of September 2020, they have awarded over $2.2 billion in contracts to local and Indigenous companies and spent over $6 million on social investments and workforce development programs.[25]

OUR THOUGHTS: The Haisla Nation have long been leaders in building sustainable economic strategies to benefit all members of their community. The presence of LNG Canada within their traditional territories represented an extraordinary opportunity to build on that knowledge and experience and create a legacy of economic independence for their community. This is exactly what they have done.

The team at LNG Canada led by enlightened leadership who made a meaningful commitment to reconciliation, shared decision-making, and local investment and employment core to everything that they have done right from the beginning, have raised the bar on how resource companies should engage with Indigenous communities. The leadership of both the Haisla and LNG Canada deserve recognition for their effort, commitment, and execution of this major investment and the partnerships that have been formed here.

Case Study Five: Tahltan Nation and Newcrest Mining

The Tahltan Nation's Territory spans 95,933 square kilometres of northwest BC, or the equivalent of 11 percent of the province. Within that territory is an operating copper-gold mine known as Red Chris. This mine is owned by Newcrest Mining of Australia and Imperial Metals of Vancouver. In recent engineering studies, the Red Chris project is predicted to have a life of another thirty-one years, or out to past 2050.

ABOUT THE TAHLTAN: The Tahltan Central Government (TCG) is the administrative governing body of the Tahltan Nation. The Iskut Band and the Tahltan Band continue to govern Tahltan interests with respect to the Indian Act in the communities of Iskut, Dease Lake, and Telegraph Creek.

The TCG is the representative government of the Tahltan Nation with respect to the inherent and collective Aboriginal title and rights shared by all Tahltan people.

Tahltan culture is organized through a matrilinear clan system. This means that crests and inheritance are passed down through the mother. Since time immemorial, this system has provided the basis of Tahltan law and governance. Despite the imposition of a settler society form of government (through the Indian Act), the matrilineal system remains the foundational governing structure of the Tahltan people.

The Tahltan Nation is divided into two clans, the Crow (or Tsesk'iya) and the Wolf (or Ch'ioyone). Each clan is further divided into several family groups. Legends about the Crow and Raven continue to guide the Tahltan people about the best way of living, for example, by the principles of determination, generosity, and resourcefulness, among others.

ABOUT NEWCREST: Newcrest is the largest gold producer listed on the Australian Securities Exchange and one of the world's largest gold mining companies. Their headquarters are in Melbourne, and they have operating mines in Australia, Canada, and Papua New Guinea.

Newcrest acquired a 70 percent interest in Red Chris in August 2019. At the time of acquisition, Newcrest and the TCG signed an updated Impact, Benefit, and Co-Management Agreement (IBCA), which covers contracting and business development opportunities, among other things.

ECONOMIC BENEFITS OF RED CHRIS TO THE TAHLTAN NATION: Implementation of the IBCA requires agreement between the parties on how to best harness and build local enterprises and skills. To facilitate this, in FY20, Newcrest expended approximately CAD$43 million on contracts with Tahltan entities.

Newcrest reports that they are working to develop enduring partnerships with Tahltan businesses to support continued economic and business development within Tahltan territory. For example, Tahltan Forestry provides logging services to Red Chris to log areas required for future mine development. Tahltan Forestry also sells logs acquired from the Red Chris site; they have delivered logs to the communities of Iskut, Dease Lake, and Telegraph Creek for firewood.

The Tahltan Nation Development Corporation provides airport services at Dease Lake, including aircraft de-icing. This improves the transport reliability for our workforce and aligns with the mutual vision of Newcrest and the Tahltan Central Government to improve private and commercial air services to the region.

As well as partnering with the larger Tahltan businesses, Newcrest is working to improve the contracting of small local businesses such as Kica Contracting, which supplies catering and housekeeping services to the overflow camp at Red Chris. Newcrest has also contracted Dease Lake Super A Foods to supply food to the catering company that services the temporary accommodation.

Newcrest reports that they employ approximately 220 Tahltan people, either directly or through their business partners. In addition, around 50 percent of apprentices at Red Chris are Tahltan.

OUR THOUGHTS: Both of us have had the good fortune to work with the Tahltan for many years. There are so many great things to say about the strength and vision of the Tahltan people, and this relationship with Newcrest is just another example of that.

The Tahltan people understand resources and mining and for many decades have ensured that their people are front and centre in decisions being made that have the potential to affect them. The Red Chris project is a multigenerational opportunity that is providing significant economic benefits to the Tahltan Nation, and we expect to see more innovative ideas for sustainable development in the years ahead.[26,27]

Case Study Six: The Cariboo Gold Project, Osisko Development Corporation, and the Lhtako Dené Nation

The Cariboo Gold Project (CGP) is currently proceeding through a comprehensive environmental assessment under the British Columbia Environmental Assessment process. The project is a proposed underground gold mine and milling operation located in the Cariboo region of central BC near the towns of Wells and Quesnel. The proposed project is building on a long history of gold mining in the area that dates back to the 1800s, when prospectors and explorers first came to western Canada in search of mineral riches.

OSISKO DEVELOPMENT CORPORATION (OSISKO): Osisko is a Canadian mine developer headquartered in Montreal. The company is publicly traded on the Toronto Stock Exchange and is the proponent of the Cariboo Gold Project. Cariboo Gold is intended to be an underground gold mine that will operate initially at 4,750 tonnes per day. It will have an estimated operational mine life of sixteen years, with an overall mine life of approximately twenty-five to thirty-five years (construction through post-closure). Initial capital costs (capex) are reported to be CAD$433 million, and the mine will support 459 direct jobs in operations and a further 273 jobs during construction.[28]

Osisko has built positive relations with the Lhtako Dené Nation that culminated with the signing of a comprehensive Impact Benefit Agreement in July 2021. The company also enjoys positive relationships with the Xatsull and Williams Lake First Nations and is actively working with both on a number of fronts associated with the Cariboo Gold Project and ongoing exploration and mining activities. Positive engagement, recognition of Indigenous rights, and a commitment to strong environmental protection and stewardship have been core to Osisko's work in the province up until now, and those values have translated into constructive working relationships with First Nations in the region.

LHTAKO DENÉ NATION: The Lhtako Dené Nation, known as the Quesnel Indian Band prior to 1988 and as the Red Bluff

Indian Band from 1988 to 2010, is located near the City of Quesnel. The Lhtako Dené people speak the Dakelh language and are referred to as the "Carrier," "Southern Carrier," or "Southern Dakelh" people.

In general, the Dakelh people have occupied the vast area encompassing Barkerville, Wells, and the Bowron Lakes region since time immemorial. There is strong evidence demonstrating pre-contact patterns of use and occupation, which continue to the present.

PARTNERSHIP IN DEVELOPMENT: Osisko and the Lhtako Dené have a working relationship that has several benefits that are enjoyed by both. Osisko has an actively engaged Indigenous partner who is willing to work with the company collaboratively in the design, permitting, and ultimate development of the Cariboo Gold Project. And for the Lhtako Dené, their community benefits through material economic benefits, including funding, employment, contracting, and business development. By being actively engaged in the ongoing environmental assessment, permitting, and monitoring of the environment in their territory, the Lhtako Dené are also ensuring the health and protection of their people for this and future generations.

OUR THOUGHTS: Both of us have been working with the Osisko team for the last several years since it acquired the company known as Barkerville Gold Mines, which used to own the mining properties in the area. Osisko has made Indigenous engagement a cornerstone of its work in the province, and the team has done an excellent job—both in addressing concerns as they are raised and investing in the future to the benefit of the First Nations in the area. A public statement from the chief of Lhtako Dené on October 27, 2021, in response to the

Province of BC issuing permits for Osisko's mine operations in the area, attest to this:

> This partnership illustrates that First Nations and industry can work together in a good way for the benefit of both partners, economically and with community growth for Wells, Quesnel and the Lhtako Dené Nation. It's more than jobs and contract opportunities or training, it's the development and growth of all three communities and all the ones in between that is important here. The Lhtako Dené Nation looks forward to working together with Osisko Development Corporation in the future to move these values forward.

This has been a great example of how to do things well, and both parties in this relationship deserve congratulations and support for advancing a good project in a way that provides real, sustainable benefits to their nation, the Province of BC, and Canada.

Indigenomics and the Future

Indigenomics is the study of the economic systems of Indigenous Peoples. It is a term used increasingly in the dialogue around the opportunities associated with Indigenous-led economic development. If you are interested in learning more about this, we recommend you check out a newly created Canadian organization called the Indigenomics Institute and the author Carol Anne Hilton.[29]

The discussion with the Indigenomics Institute is about Indigenous economies associated with a variety of industries and businesses. There is reference to the CAD$100 billion in opportunities they can see for Aboriginal businesses to take part in and the untapped potential of a young, vibrant part of the population. It is all great stuff and worth considering because, again, it is about where things could go and are going. So much is happening today that it is almost hard to keep up.

From a natural resource economy perspective, the common denominator is that the lands on which major resource projects are taking place or are being proposed are often either on or in close proximity to Indigenous communities. That is the case in Canada, in much of the US, in Central and South America, and in other parts of the world.

And, as we discussed earlier, the scale of economic opportunity associated with the various resource industries is massive, from the exploration and discovery of mineral deposits to their ultimate extraction—or being a supplier to the resource sector broadly by providing equipment, professional support, advice, or goods and services. These are multi-billion-dollar enterprises and opportunities that can be pursued.

But as we know, getting from where we are today to the meaningful involvement of Indigenous Peoples, Indigenous communities, and Indigenous-owned and -led businesses becoming real players in these multi-billion-dollar industries will not happen overnight or easily.

There are big established companies that currently dominate these business sectors, with tremendous power, influence, and resources at their disposal. And, as we have seen with regard to resistance to responding to major issues like climate change, these same companies and industries can be slow to change and adapt—or, let's be honest, share in the bounty that they have made their wealth from for a very long time.

Most of the businesses involved have a core mandate of returning maximum value to their shareholders. This means that sharing or "giving up" what they already have is difficult to do sometimes, regardless of what any particular enlightened

CEO or management team member might want to do. This is not to say that that some will not take the right road here and make changes, work to open up markets to Indigenous businesses, or make the extra effort to build capacity. The case studies we mentioned earlier show that some leading companies and Indigenous communities are making steps toward economic reconciliation. It just means that, in so doing, these ventures and initiatives need to overcome the gravitational pull of traditional capitalist systems that focus more on traditional structures and definitions of what an acceptable "return" is than on greater societal health and well-being.

There are also significant barriers to Indigenous communities becoming involved in global-scale businesses such as the resource industry—access to capital being a major one, but also having the people with the right experience to run major projects or companies. These are big, complex undertakings with organizations and industries that have evolved over the past century and a half or longer.

So, it will take a little time.

But if progress is to be made, the key is to see things moving forward—which, we believe, is happening. There are plenty of examples in recent years of partnerships, of joint ventures, and of Indigenous-led enterprises that are changing the landscape of how things are done, as we have given readers a sample of. And we only see that accelerating in the months and years ahead—because, in our view, true reconciliation can only come when Indigenous leaders are fully at the table where decisions are being made. It does not come from engagement and consultation on its own. It comes from being respected as equals and from participating in decision-making over issues that affect their people and their communities and being empowered to make decisions about the future of lands, waters, and resources so that future generations will have the safety of a clean environment and the opportunity of a vibrant economy.

For the current leaders of the extractive industry, this is your opportunity to be allies in the pursuit of reconciliation and equality. To embed the ideas of allyship into your organization and empower your executive and management teams to try things. Be innovative. Remove the barriers that have prevented progress from happening. Be the people without racist attitudes or needless bureaucracy that stifles new ways of doing things. That is your obligation, and if you truly want to make a difference, then begin with your own organization; start with self-reflection and learn from that. Then take what you have learned and make the changes that are necessary to move things forward.

The opportunities are extraordinary and, in some cases, just seem like common sense. Why would resource companies not be owned and operated by Indigenous leaders? Why shouldn't the major contractors to the resource sector not be Indigenous-owned and -led? If there are trillions of dollars in economic value being created annually from the activities of the resource sector globally, why shouldn't a material portion of that go directly to supporting Indigenous businesses, communities, and their ultimate well-being, given that those resources are being extracted from lands on which they have a legitimate interest?

Final Thoughts

We know this is the part of the book where we are supposed to end with opportunity and enthusiasm, that if we just get this right, it will all be rainbows and unicorns. Indigenous-led resource companies, full employment, and social issues such as low graduation rates and the scars of residential schools and colonization will be addressed and fade into the background. We hope that we will get the balance between economic development and environmental stewardship right, and that through wise investments, our carbon emissions will drop and the global climate systems will be protected against further degradation.

But most of us know that to get to those places will take a lot of hard work, and it will not happen in a straight line.

Where we are today is not going to change quickly, and there is a lot of work to do to establish the foundations for making economic reconciliation possible. Which is why we are both a little cautious when we hear all this talk of hundreds of billions of dollars in opportunities for Indigenous-led businesses. Yes, those opportunities are there, for sure. But how do we get from where we are today to realizing that? And how do we not make the mistake of not doing the hard work necessary to strengthen Indigenous communities, repair the harm that was done from the not-so-distant colonial history of subjugation, and support the transition to fully sustainable economies with meaningful Indigenous participation?

This is where the idea of resource companies being allies in this pursuit comes to ground. We believe that resource companies with enlightened leadership can help bridge the gap between where we are today and what is possible when it comes to indigenomics. And it is through allyship and a focus on reconciliation, through an active commitment to supporting the development of new businesses and new Indigenous-led enterprises, that indigenomics can be made real.

And finally, we all live on one planet Earth. Whether Indigenous or non-Indigenous, we all breath the same air, drink the same water, and rely on Mother Nature to provide for our well-being. As we have discussed, we have often not given what is provided for us the respect it deserves, and that hurts all of us. By being allies with Indigenous communities, we have an opportunity to rediscover a balance that provides not only for our well-being today but for future generations.

Acknowledgements

Christy

I would like to humbly acknowledge and raise my hands to the Creator and my ancestors, those who advocated before me, those who provided my voice in this book. Writing a book was on my bucket list, and it was unexpectedly extremely intimidating. I thank Mike for always believing in me and giving me that kick in the pants to start writing. The journey to place words on paper and then share it with the world could not have been done without all of the relationships I have with family, friends, and colleagues—you know who you are, and I love you all. Specifically, it is with profound love that I thank Jason Hadath for being my greatest fan and supporter; Jen Gebert for her amazing friendship and being there daily to listen to me; and Melinda Knox, K'ómoks Matriarch, for her big Auntie energy and continuous love. A huge shout-out to Ta7talíya Nahanee from Nahanee Creative Inc. for her work on the front cover.

Mike

First, I would like to acknowledge my co-author of this work, Christy. A remarkable leader, woman, mother, colleague, and friend. I have learned so much from her over the years and consider it a privilege to have had the opportunity to put these words down with her. I would also like to thank all the people who gave their time and insights in helping to create this work. A specific acknowledgment to Anthony Hodge, Jim Cooney, Jessica McDonald, Sean Roosen, Stephen D'esposito, Colin Webster, and Francois Vezina. Our team at Falkirk Environmental also deserves mention for their support and inspiration in our work.

Finally, to the amazing people around me who support me always in what I do and without whom I would not be able to do any of this. My family, specifically my boys, Henry, Matthew, and Oskar, who inspire me every day; my mom and dad, who have helped shape the values that drive my work; and Susan Dolnik, who has been by my side through many hours of trying to get this right.

FINALLY, WE would both like to sincerely thank the Page Two team who have nurtured, guided, advised, and supported us through this journey. Jesse Finkelstein, Amanda Lewis, Melissa Kawaguchi, Christine Savage, Chris Brandt, Jessica Werb, and Peter Cocking. You are remarkable professionals and people, and we appreciate everything that you have done for us in this.

Notes

1. Marie-Danielle Smith, "Murray Sinclair on reconciliation, anger, unmarked graves—and a headline for this story," *Maclean's*, August 18, 2021, macleans.ca/longforms/murray-sinclair-on-reconciliation-anger-unmarked-graves-and-a-headline-for-this-story/.

2. "Goal 12: Responsible Consumption and Production," United Nations Department of Economic and Social Affairs, Statistics Division, unstats.un.org/sdgs/report/2019/goal-12.

3. "Global Pension Statistics," OECD, November 11, 2021, oecd.org/finance/private-pensions/globalpensionstatistics.htm.

4. Dr. Pragya Agarwal, "Unconscious Bias: How It Affects Us More Than We Know," *Forbes*, December 3, 2018, forbes.com/sites/pragyaagarwaleurope/2018/12/03/unconscious-bias-how-it-affects-us-more-than-we-know.

5. Douglas Starr, "The Bias Detective," *Science*, March 26, 2020, science.org/content/article/meet-psychologist-exploring-unconscious-bias-and-its-tragic-consequences-society.

6. "Royal Proclamation, 1763," Indigenous Foundations, First Nations & Indigenous Studies, University of British Columbia, indigenousfoundations.arts.ubc.ca/royal_proclamation_1763/.

7. "The Aboriginal languages of First Nations people, Métis and Inuit," Statistics Canada, October 25, 2017, www12.statcan.gc.ca/census-recensement/2016/as-sa/98-200-x/2016022/98-200-x2016022-eng.cfm.

8. Truth and Reconciliation Commission of Canada, *Honouring the Truth, Reconciling for the Future: Summary of the Final Report of the Truth and Reconciliation Commission of Canada*, 2015.

9. "Indigenous Peoples and Mining: Position Statement," ICMM, 2013, icmm.com/en-gb/about-us/member-requirements/position-statements/indigenous-peoples.

10. "Honouring Water," Assembly of the First Nations, afn.ca/honoring-water/.

11. Julian T. Inglis, Ed., *Traditional Ecological Knowledge Concepts and Cases* (Ottawa, ON: 1993), idrc.ca/sites/default/files/openebooks/683-6/index.html.

12. Lauren E. Eckert et al., "Indigenous Knowledge and Federal Environmental Assessments in Canada: Applying Past Lessons to 2019 Impact Assessment Act," *FACETS*, February 13, 2020, doi. org/10.1139/facets-2019-0039.

13. "Traditional Knowledge," Assembly of the First Nations, afn.ca/uploads/files/env/ns_-_traditional_knowledge.pdf.

14. "What is the Seventh Generation Principle?" *Indigenous Corporate Training Inc.* (blog), May 30, 2020, ictinc.ca/blog/seventh-generation-principle.

15. Anastasia Shkilnyk, *A Poison Stronger than Love: The Destruction of an Ojibwa Community* (New Haven, CT: Yale University Press, 1985).

16. Adam Mosa and Jacalyn Duffin, "The Interwoven History of Mercury Poisoning in Ontario and Japan," *CMAJ*, February 7, 2017, doi. org/10.1503/cmaj.160943.

17. The global mining market consists of sales of minerals, metals, and other valuable materials such as sand and gravel, coal, and stone extracted from the earth's crust by entities (organizations, sole traders, and partnerships) that undertake the process of extraction. The mining market is segmented into mining services; general minerals; stones; copper, nickel, lead, and zinc; metal ore; and coal, lignite, and anthracite. Source: *Mining Global Market Report 2021: COVID-19 Impact and Recovery to 2030*, Business Research Comapany, January 2021, researchandmarkets.com/reports/5240246.

18. "About," Mineral Choices, mineral-choices.com/about.

19. "World Energy Investment 2021," IEA, 2021, iea.org/reports/world-energy-investment-2021/executive-summary.

20. "Western Forest Products Inc. Completes Sale of an Incremental Ownership Interest in TFL 44 LP to Huumiis Ventures LP," CISION, May 3, 2021, newswire.ca/news-releases/western-forest-products-inc-completes-sale-of-an-incremental-ownership-interest-in-tfl-44-lp-to-huumiis-ventures-lp-817828000.html.
21. LNG Canada, lngcanada.ca/.
22. "Benefiting the Local Community and Creating Indigenous Opportunities," LNG Canada, September 17, 2021, lngcanada.ca/news/benefiting-the-local-community-and-creating-indigenous-opportunities/.
23. "Indigenous Relations," Coastal GasLink, coastalgaslink.com/sustainability/indigenous-relations/.
24. Matt Robinson, "LNG Canada Set 'New Standard' for First Nations Consultation," *Vancouver Sun*, October 3, 2018, vancouversun.com/news/local-news/lng-canada-set-new-standard-for-first-nations-consultation; Lee Wilson, "Haisla Nation to benefit From Tugboat Contract Associated with LNG Pipeline," *National News*, September 13, 2019, aptnnews.ca/national-news/haisla-nation-to-benefit-from-tugboat-contract-associated-with-lng-pipeline/.
25. "Benefiting the Local Community and Creating Indigenous Opportunities," LNG Canada, September 17, 2021, lngcanada.ca/news/benefiting-the-local-community-and-creating-indigenous-opportunities/.
26. "Culture," Tahltan Central Government, tahltan.org/culture-heritage/.
27. "Tahltan Are Delivering the Goods for Red Chris," Newcrest Mining Limited, newcrest.com/tahltan-are-delivering-goods-red-chris.
28. "Cariboo Gold Project," Government of British Columbia, projects.eao.gov.bc.ca/p/5d40cc5b4cb2c7001b1336b8/project-details.
29. Indigenomics Institute, indigenomicsinstitute.com.

About
the Authors

Christy Smith

Christy Smith is a member of K'ómoks First Nation living in her traditional territory on Vancouver Island. Being bicultural has allowed Christy to authentically navigate both Indigenous and non-Indigenous worlds while working in the resource sector for over twenty-five years. Engaging and building good relationships are at the core of what Christy does as a change-maker, mentor, liaison, project manager, and engagement expert. She has facilitated workshops, presented at national mining conventions, instructed at universities, de-escalated complex situations, mentored Indigenous entrepreneurs, nego-tiated countless benefits agreements, advocated on behalf of First Nations governments and industry proponents, and built capacity within every organization of which she has been a part. Christy currently serves as a partner and vice president, Indigenous and Stakeholder Relations, with Falkirk Environ-mental Consultants Ltd. of Vancouver and vice president, Sustainability, with TDG Gold Corp.

Michael McPhie

Michael McPhie is an executive with more than twenty-five years of experience in the Canadian and international resource industry. Over his career he has been a CEO, chairman of the board, founder, partner, and officer of public and private companies. Michael currently serves as a founding partner and co-chair of Falkirk Environmental, where he acts as a senior advisor to resource companies, governments, and communities and is on the board and an officer of several Canadian public mineral exploration and mining companies. He is also a member of the Board of Advisors of the Washington, DC–based non-governmental organization Resolve.

Michael is former chair of the boards of Ridley Terminals Inc., the British Columbia Institute of Technology (BCIT), and the Association for Mineral Exploration BC (AME). He is also former president and CEO of the Mining Association of British Columbia. He lives in Vancouver, BC.

Get in Touch with the Authors

THANKS FOR reading *Weaving Two Worlds*. We hope you enjoyed it. This is, in many ways, a book about our life's work helping resource companies and their management teams build positive, constructive relationships with communities. If either or both of us can help you or your organization, please get in touch. We would love to connect with you!

Visit our book website at weavingtwoworlds.com.

Learn more about our company, Falkirk Environmental Consultants, at falkirk.ca.

Find us on social media

- 🔗 Mike: linkedin.com/in/michael-mcphie-78934710/
- 🔗 Christy: linkedin.com/in/christy-smith-50b81620/
- 🔗 Falkirk: linkedin.com/in/falkirk-environmental-consultants-ltd-179364102/
- 🐦 @michaelmcphie
- 📷 @christy_smith_komoks

Reach out!

Mike: E: mike@falkirk.ca; M: 1-778-772-0528
Christy: E: christy@falkirk.ca; M: 1-250-267-8989

Like this book? We would appreciate a review on your preferred online retailer.

Scan this QR code and leave a review.

This book is also available as an ebook.

Manufactured by Amazon.ca
Bolton, ON

26408758R00109